Glo
and CUBA-U.S.
Conflict

About the Authors

GRACIELA CHAILLOUX LAFFITA (Havana, 1949). Ph.D. History Sciences, Universidad de La Habana, 1988. Titular researcher. She has made research studies and been a pre- and postgraduate professor of Cuban economic thought, economic history of Cuba, and Cuba-U.S. relations. Doctor Chailloux has been a tutor, opponent, and member of the board of examiners for diploma works and doctorate theses. She has presented papers at national and international scientific events, and has lectured at Cuban, U.S., and Spanish universities. *Historia económica de Cuba* (Economic History of Cuba) (1983), and *José Martí frente al imperialismo norteamericano* (José Martí Facing U.S. imperialism) (1990) are among her books. She has also published papers in Cuba and abroad.

ROSA LÓPEZ OCEGUERA (Havana, 1947). History professor, 1976. A Doctor in History Sciences to be. She has been a pre- and post graduate professor of U.S. foreign policy, and Cuba-U.S. relations. She has presented papers at national and international scientific events, and has lectured at Cuban and U.S. universities. Professor López's works have been published both in Cuba and abroad. One of her most significant researches is La guerra fría: contexto de la relación Estados Unidos-Cuba-Unión Soviética (Cold War—Context of U.S.- Cuba-Soviet Union Relations).

SILVIO BARÓ HERRERA (Havana, 1944). Ph.D. Economic Sciences, Universidad de La Habana, 1988. Titular researcher. He has made research studies and been a pre- and postgraduate professor of political economy, universal economic thought, and international economic relations. Doctor Baró has been a tutor, opponent, and member of the board of examiners for diploma works and doctorate theses while being an expert on economic development and underdevelopment. He has presented papers at national and international scientific events, and has acted as an expert at forums of international institutions—4th UNCTAD Conference, 1983; VII Congreso de la Asociación Internacional de Economía, (7th International Economy Association Congress); 1983 World Summit on Social Development, 1995. *El nuevo orden económico internacional: antecedentes, problemas actuales y perspectivas* (The New International Economic Order—Background, Current Trends and Perspectives) is among his books. Doctor Baró has also published papers in Cuba and abroad.

Globalization and CUBA-U.S. Conflict

Graciela Chailloux Laffita
Rosa López Oceguera
Silvio Baró Herrera

Editorial JOSÉ MARTÍ

Original title in Spanish:
Globalización y conflicto Cuba-Estados Unidos
Translation: Frank Cabrera
Editing: Mayra Fernández, Rubén Casado and Martha Acosta
Cover design: Santiago Ramírez Pérez
Design and composition: Ileana Álvarez Verdecia

I.S.B.N.: 959-09-0142-5
Depósito Legal: M-34438-1999
Imprime: S.S.A.G., S.L. - MADRID (España)
Tel.: 34-91 797 37 09 - Fax: 34-91 797 37 73

INSTITUTO CUBANO DEL LIBRO
Editorial JOSÉ MARTÍ
Publicaciones en Lenguas Extranjeras
Calzada No. 259 e/ J e I, Vedado
Ciudad de La Habana, Cuba

Contents

Introduction

For the analysis of the relations between Cuba and the United States, the relevance and significance of the North-South problem are increasingly stressed as the last decade of the 20th century proceeds and the international system, instead of simplifying itself once the Cold War ended, becomes more complex.

The disappearance of the East-West conflict deprived the scholars on international relations of the paradigmatic analysis model that, for almost half a century, had enabled them to explain the diverse phenomena and events in this field from the prevailing arrangement in the worldwide context, leaving them without a theoretical and methodological basis. The vertiginous changes that occurred at the end of the eighties and the beginning of the nineties also demolished conceptual structures together with the Berlin Wall.

The impossibility to continue studying the world by the old patterns of thought forces the social scientist not only to form a new concept of reality in order to approach it in all its richness and to find explanations for the new phenomena appearing in the international context but also to reevaluate past processes and stages—previously focused from other points of view and understood from other assumptions that do not comply with the needs of both theory and practice any longer. Because of this, the reader of the present study will face a piece of work that does not pretend to qualify the processes under analysis in definitive terms.

Consequently, since the subject was first approached the authors have tried to show, in all its richness and complexity, the transition of the present system of international relations and its many-sided implications regarding Cuba-U.S. relations. Such a purpose has been identified considering the feature of the subject matter: its transitional character. As a result of that, we have worked guided by the interest of contributing to the recognition of the methodological and conceptual fundamentals for the study of the matter in question. The Cuban Nation's reconstruction project requires scientific knowledge of the global reality where it takes place, and also of the steps taken by the United States to retain the global leadership and hegemony they have been enjoying—although substantially eroded—since the end of World War II. That is why the reader is faced with a work that is just a starting point which cannot be dispensed with.

Since the revolutionary triumph in 1959, Cuba-U.S. relations were both objectively and subjectively framed within the confrontation between superpowers—an approach which tended to disregard the rest of the problems included in the historical conflict involving a small Caribbean country and the hemisphere's colossus—in spite of the fact that the underlying and dynamics-expressed matters under dispute had little or nothing to do with the strategic rivalry between the United States and the USSR—beyond the international conditions in which they evolved—but had a lot to do with the leading subjects (sovereignty, self-determination, right to development, and so on) of the North/South contradiction at that historical-concrete moment.

However, a scientific analysis of the relations between Cuba and the United States either by taking into account its historical dimension or its status quo must consider the two aspects of the conflict: the one derived from its relevance to the confrontation prompting the evolvement of the contradiction between two opposing socioeconomic systems, and the one governing the interrelation between the big countries and the small ones, the developed countries and the underdeveloped ones.

That is the reason why the conceptualizations on the brand-new phenomenon of globalization are put under study as it is indispensable to establish clearly and precisely the meaning of that category. References to the globalization process are commonly found—in which it is defined as a new problem of economic dimensions, detached from the general trends that have historically encouraged the evolvement of the capitalist production system.

The first chapter of the present study clarifies the particular and the general sides of the globalization process understood as a stage in the internationalization process characterizing the capitalist development since it began in the late 15th century. Besides, globalization is considered as a process with both economic and political dimensions, a feature that typifies it as the first moment of internationalization. The countries forming the core of the system may then consider to implement a design towards the building up of global conditions where their hegemony reigns not only in economic terms but also in political ones amounting to economic dominance. Current considerations born in the seventies on the relation between development and underdevelopment, and the theoretical and conceptual context in which the search for scientific knowledge on globalization evolves, are also contents of the first chapter.

The second chapter, "Worldwide Trends and North-South Relations," is aimed at explaining the likely implications of the globalization process in Cuba-U.S. relations. In this sense, new world trends have been studied to show how processes that occur nowadays—and that are frequently considered as devoid of connection—are manifestations of a unique, general phenomenon, but a multidimensional one.

Consequently, scientific-technical progress, new manifestations in the realm of international economic relations, recent global behavior within the social order, the link established between ecology and globalization, newly-born political conceptions with pretensions of universality, and the appearance of political trends trying to homogenize the human society from paradigms and institutions that serve the interests of the "centers," are the elements that qualify, both objectively and subjectively, the present stage of capitalist evolvement in which the North-South confrontation will be present—as it has ever been in the preceding stages of capitalist development.

Once the bipolar confrontation headed by the former USSR and the United States ended, the latter is prone to attain universal leadership and hegemony. But to gain it, modifications in the essence of the fundamentals that formerly originated the international U.S. projection are required. To that aim, the U.S. political and academic circles have to comply with the requisite of defining, within the new international context announced, the fresh contents of their concept of national security, and also the domestic and foreign imperatives it demands.

Issues like the trends of the U.S. debate on "Attaining Leadership and Hegemony in the New World Order," heading of the third chapter, are discussed in the present study. It also approaches the most distinguishing features of the foreign policy during the

William Clinton administration, the first one of the post-Cold War era. The subject about the role and place of Latin America within the U.S. foreign policy in the near future is dealt with in both items as, from that geographic area, the United States plans their standing of potency and hegemony. Besides, it is the place of Cuba in world geography whose privileged site has enabled the Island to achieve its new articulation within the international system of relations.

Finally, in the fourth chapter the relation of the international context, the U.S. foreign policy trends and the reinsertion process of Cuba in international relations is analyzed—rather to bring up the existing problems than to define potential future trends. Establishing the historical character of the confrontational relationship between Cuba and the United States has enabled to separate the conjuncture component from the regular one of the aforementioned conflict within the ambit of the universal North-South confrontation.

The purpose of this study has been to emphasize the North-South aspect of the Cuba-U.S. conflict, viewed in its present expression and focusing on the U.S. projections towards not only the rest of the hemisphere but also what was known as Third World when there were bipolarity conditions. The historical aspects and the peculiarities of that problem during the prerevolutionary period—studied by diverse authors,[1] especially on the issue of economic dependency and political subordination—will not be examined. References to the period be-

1. For a review on the conditions of neocolonialism in Cuba, refer to Julio Le Riverend, *Historia económica de Cuba* (La Habana: Editorial de Ciencias Sociales, 1985); Leland H. Jenks, *Nuestra colonia de Cuba* (La Habana: Edición Revolucionaria, 1966); Francisca López Civeira, comp., *Historia de las relaciones de Estados Unidos con Cuba* (La Habana: Ministerio de Educación Superior, 1985).

fore 1959 will only be made when absolutely necessary for the analysis in question.

Lastly, it is restated that the core of this study is to contribute to the collective effort—necessarily a multidisciplinary one—to set the methodological basis and the category system enabling to follow the trends the transition process of the system of international relations is going through, in which there are extremely new and opposing trends. Their knowledge cannot be postponed because it is required not only for the necessary updating of the Cuban social sciences but also for the political practice of a country approaching an imminent redefinition of its national project facing the world.

The authors wish to state that the printing of this work has been possible thanks to the financing rendered by the University of Havana. This institution held the contest "Alma Mater 95" where this research project was awarded.

From Internationalization to Globalization

From Internationalization to Transnationalization

During the Cold War period, North-South contradictions were subordinated to the fundamental contradiction among the nuclear superpowers, and no element or subsystem of the system of international relations could evade itself from the conditions this confrontational logic had created. But in spite of that they still existed although their action was sometimes deemed as an East-West contradiction.

Once World War II ended, an era of U.S. supremacy in the international relations started. This hegemony was challenged by the USSR. During this period however a decolonization process—by means of which a number of territories in Asia, Africa and the Caribbean gained independence—also took place, and the search for economic and political alternatives which satisfied the aspirations of the majorities was activated.

In this context, dichotomous concepts like development-underdevelopment, North-South, center-periphery were born. They were used according to the aspects stressed in debates, thus showing the diversity of the phenomenon in itself. This diversity is not exhausted by economic or geographical issues nor by the political/military alignment/non-alignment of the parties, but it involves a huge blend of complex problems dating back to colonial and neocolonial relations—both among and within different regions of the world—as well as the many-sided deformations these relations generated within the structures of societies. Their evolution was determined from abroad. The situation is valid for most nations, except the most industrialized ones.

The so-called North-South contradictions precede by far any arrangement made during the present century—although they did not have the features they currently show. These contradictions are the permanent context in which the relations between a fourth of humanity and the remaining three fourths evolve, so in terms of universality they are the most spread while being the most persistent as far as unapproachability is concerned. Consequently North-South contradictions hold an outstanding status in the international system although people do not realize the fact.

Besides it must be remembered that the North-South problem—not only in its origins but also along its evolution—manifests in the capitalist mode of production. The forces behind the newly-born system drove the approach of Europe to the rest of the world. The "backward" and "non-Christian" regions played a key role in the process of original accumulation of capital. The primordial patterns of distribution of world power were thus established, and still exist.

The capitalist mode of production has always been international. Firstly because its earliest symptoms became evident in some nations of the present western Europe more or less simultaneously. Secondly because the process aimed at extensive development and consolidation of capitalist relations of production progressed from the process of original accumulation of capital which involved the extraction of wealth from some parts of the world to assure the aim in others.

Therefore, since its origins the internationalization of the economic activity is a phenomenon that has been accompanying the capitalist development along each and every phase it has gone through. Consequently the evolvement of this phenomenon is a relevant element for the analysis of the North-South problem nowadays. In order to study this problem it must be taken into account that it occurs within the globalization processes which are considered the present stage of internationalization.

Although internationalizaton—understood as leading the economic relations beyond the borders of a given state—is born together with simple merchant-production, it gained both its relevant character and close interrelationship with the production mechanisms only with the advent of capitalism.[2]

Then its evolution is related to the diverse stages the capitalist system has gone through. To each of these stages corresponds a certain level of technological development, a certain way of production organization, and the leadership of a country or group of countries.[3] The geographic discoveries made in the last decades of the 15th century and the beginning of the 16th, aided by the progress achieved in navigation and weaponry, meant the apotheosis of mercantilism. It expanded trade both within Europe and on the Mediterranean Sea towards regions of the world formerly unexplored while propelling an already-existing dynamics that lead to the predominance of capitalism as mode of production, the appearance of national states, and the creation of the world system.

2. Silvio Baró Herrera, "Globalización y exclusión: dos tendencias en la economía mundial", 1992. Typescript.
3. John H. Dunning, *Globalization, Economic Restructuring and Development* (Geneva: UNCTAD, 1994), 5.

The opportunity the European powers had—firstly Spain and Portugal and then France, England and Holland—to exploit the natural resources and mainly the work force in vast regions of the planet to serve their interests laid the foundations for what we nowadays call "North-South relations." These are distinguished by a ferocious reconcentration of worldwide economic resources controlled by the "center" or "North." North-South relations have essentially remained unchanged regardless the diverse forms they have adopted for five hundred years.

However, what has been more recently called *internationalization* has been present since late 19th century, but it is more characteristic of the 20th. This internationalization of capitalist production relations was generated by two parallel and closely-related processes. On the one hand, a forceful development of production forces resulting from the accumulation of a number of inventions and research findings which could more or less readily be applied to production, and rendered remarkable output growth and increase in labor productivity. It also meant the introduction of important modifications into the production structures in nations where capitalism had evolved. It might be said that the capitalist mode of production—until then characterized by the presence of medium-sized companies and small ones mainly in the field of light industry—started to be identified by the construction and operation of big companies mainly in the heavy-industry field. On the other hand, the period under analysis likewise featured an even greater consolidation of capitalist production relations in the developed countries—on their way to imperialism—and the promotion of such relations in the colonies and semicolonies dominated by them. As with technology, the new environment was characterized by both a quantitative and qualitative transformation of capitalist production relations.

The convergence of both processes helped forming the capitalist system of world economy. It is then when one may properly talk about internationalization of the capitalist mode of production and internationalization of its production relations.

Unlike the "initial internationalization" in the dawn of the capitalist mode of production, it became a question of international expansion of the production relations and the rest of the operative features of the system due to the fact that the countries were completely connected not by subtle and unstable commercial links but by a broad and many-sided network of bonds.

Production started to internationalize. Capital exporting and the economic and territorial distribution of the world lead to the fact that the natural resources and even the work force of some countries became subjected to the development of the production activity in others. A rather well-defined international and capitalist division of work—according to which the developed countries would specialize in producing and exporting manufactured goods while the underdeveloped ones (colonial territories, semicolonial and dependant countries) would do in raw materials and half-elaborated products—would be established. In the commerce field, production output determined a rise in the relative importance of foreign markets to realize production, to value invested capital, and to reproduce particular economies. In the field of international monetary and financial circulation, internationalization manifested through capital exporting, i.e., investment-and-loan flows from developed countries to underdeveloped ones by means of which the former were able to control and subject the latter.

Internationalization was also evident by the relevance given to certain national currencies to make them act as international means of exchange.

The first century after the Industrial Revolution —from 1770 to 1875 approximately—was the era of free-concurrence capitalism characterized by the factory system, privately owned-and-managed companies, and the hegemony of Great Britain as a leader of technological processes—steam engine, mechanical force. International activity was based on availability of natural resources. When South countries participated in the world trade network, the profits rarely extended beyond some enclaves. The satisfaction of the needs of foreign buyers and customers was the reason for the existence of these territorial units.

The last quarter of the 19th century opens a new stage in capitalist development, prompted by a second industrial revolution then led by the United States, whose most outstanding technological developments were the electrical power generator, the internal-combustion engine, and precision instruments and machinery. They made the beginning of mass production of standard items possible.

The mass production system required major investments in plants, machinery, and equipment which were above individual owners' economic means. It then began a process of concentration and centralization of both production and capital that brought about the predominance of monopolies and financial capital that went beyond national or subnational level. In fact, with the transit from the free-competition to the monopolistic phase, capitalism definitively settles as a system of world economy.

During the process of internationalization, international monopolies played a decisive role because of the relevance they had on changing the national and international behavior of capitalism. Thus, V. I. Lenin considered monopolies as the main feature of imperialism, he also called monopolistic capitalism, the upper stage of capitalism. Maybe the most important question for the matter at hand is that three out of five defining characteristics of imperialism were directly related to the international expansion of the capitalist production relations.[4]

The State, in close alliance with the monopolies, directly and indirectly exercises greater activity in the domestic and foreign economic field. This brings about state monopolistic capitalism.

Just as capital exporting becomes a necessity for the reproduction of capitalism—which employs monopolies as its main agent in the economic field—, the territorial distribution of the world made by the principal powers—main cause of two world wars in the 20th century and some other armed conflicts of lesser scale—is the expression of capitalism in the political domain.

Underdeveloped countries—restricted by a static international division of labor which made them play the role of suppliers of cheap raw materials regardless their relations with the capitalist "centers"—were colonial or neocolonial.

However, it was not until World War II ended that monopolies developed all their potentialities to bring the internationalization process to an upper level. It was due to the fact that, thanks to monopolies, the sphere of production was completely internationalized and novel mechanisms appeared. By means of these mechanisms the so-called transnational companies managed to consolidate their global dominance causing important economic, social and even political consequences.

After World War II, U.S. hegemony over the world capitalist system of the world together with the technological developments in communications and transportation, and the appearance of many new independent states,

---

4. Refer to V. I. Lenin, *El imperialismo, fase superior del capitalismo* (Moscú: Editorial Progreso, n.d.).

intensified and deepened the internationalization processes of the economic activity.

The nature of international transactions was modified inasmuch as a higher rate of trade is made between nations having similar production patterns, and the specialization of the economic activity became less dependent on natural-resources distribution. Furthermore trade increasingly concentrated on transnational companies that, jointly with the broadening of their foreign operations, had tried to integrate their production and market systems.

To contend that the *transnationalization* of world economy is a higher level of internationalization is not a simple statement. Even though transnationalization is an specific case of internationalization, the former differs quantitatively and qualitatively from the latter.

Transnationalization implies a higher level of interrelation among the countries and the areas of worldwide economic life. Consequently it is a commonplace to refer to the fact that the strategies of transnational companies tend to affect the economic policies of the countries they operate in.

Foreign markets are especially nowadays more profitable for transnational companies than the markets in their own original countries, as developed as those might be. Hence transnational companies are constantly busily looking for increasingly broader markets to apply their economic strategies which imply their specific international division of labor between nations.

During this stage, a striking process of international institutionalization also emerged. It is represented by the organizations derived from the Conference of Bretton Woods and the creation of the system of the United Nations, complemented by a variety of formal and informal regional agreements, and a multitude of bilateral and multilateral arrangements.

Thus, along its development the capitalist system creates growing conditions for extending and deepening its relations. At the beginning it was geographic in character, but it progressively acquired a structural connotation.

At the beginning, internationalization was consummated through international commercial relations but would later on express itself through the internationalization of monetary and financial circulation. After Word War II, it became transnationalization when the sphere of the production was internationalized and the transnational companies were the main agents of world economy.

Globalization: A Stage of Interdependence between Nations and World Processes

For the last fifteen years now a number of trends has developed, and the fact has made many authors think the world is facing a new stage along the process of internationalization. All these processes have been conceptualized under the term *globalization* which covers not only the global-ranged phenomenon, but also the intensification of levels of interaction, interconnection and interdependence among the states and societies forming the world system.[5]

5. Among the copious bibliography than can already be referred to on the conceptualization of the globalization process, we consider the following are worth receiving special notice: G. Arroyo, "La globalización como caos"; J. Rangel, "Estados Unidos: hegemonía versus globalización"; Carlos J. Moneta, "Los probables escenarios de la globalización"; A. Toro, "Globalización y caos," *Capítulos* (SELA, Caracas) 36 (Jul.-Sept. 1993); Naúm Minsburg and H.V. Valle, eds., *El impacto de la globalización: la encrucijada económica del siglo XXI* (Buenos Aires: Ediciones Letra Buena, 1994); and A. G. McGrew and P. G. Lewis, eds., *Global Politics: Globalization and the Nation State* (Cambridge: The Polity Press, 1992), 23.

These trends follow the needs of capitalist accumulation in the present conditions, and their analysis in this study—although necessarily brief—is pertinent to understand the North-South problem in the last years of the 20th century due to their impact on international relations.

First of all, globalization typifies a number of change processes that are transforming production, trade, technology, services, and consumption patterns. These changes in capitalist economy have profound implications on both class structure and the different forms of social organization which, in their turn, modify not only the political and juridical superstructure but also the international state-centered system.

In general terms, three fundamental aspects for the analysis of capitalism—the core of the economic activity, the leadership of the system, and the relationship between economic growth and natural-resources possession—have changed considerably.

The production of goods is no longer the cardinal point of the economic activity. At present, services represent—according to World Bank data—three fifths of the Gross Domestic Product (GDP) in developed countries and almost half of it in underdeveloped ones.[6]

In the 20th century U.S. hegemony is being substituted by a triarchy of economic powers comprising United States, Japan and the European Union.

The prosperity of the countries increasingly depends less on the possession of natural resources than on know-how accumulation and the institutional capacity to efficiently organize it.

While transnationalization and internationalization were limited to the field of economic phenomena, and

6. World Bank, *World Development Report* (Oxford: University Press, 1993).

their impact on politics was secondary, oncoming globalization seems to be distinguished by the tendency to concentrate worldwide politico-economic power even more.

Nevertheless, with the advent of globalizing trends, transnational companies will neither lose their current transcendence nor drop down into a secondary position. On the contrary, many facts indicate they will keep on playing a leading role.[7]

As globalization is characterized by the search of increasingly wider politico-economic spaces, transnational companies will have a huge importance because the goals of globalization correspond to their own.

Consequently, since late last decade important modifications to the strategies and operation patterns of transnational companies are observed. Among them, the setting of a new internationalization of the productive process, and the signing of economic agreements among such companies to increase worldwide control of production, markets, financial resources, and research and development may be remarked.

However, from the above statement one must neither conclude globalization differs just in degree or intensity from transnationalization and internationalization, nor politics is more wholly brought into the scene.

Whether it is accepted that the current globalization phenomenon obeys objective laws or not, at least two approaches to the matter may be noticed.

One of them consciously or unconsciously pretends to simplify or to reduce the relevance of the phenomenon by limiting it to an economy-oriented point of view. This approach would restrict globalization to the present

7. Refer to J. M. Vidal Villa, "Diez tesis sobre la mundialización," *Memoria* (México) (Jan.-Feb. 1995).

trend of the countries to form economic and commercial blocks under the rule of the main world powers in diverse regions of the world. As it was mentioned before, globalization is thus associated to the search of increasingly wider economic spaces.[8]

Such an approach to globalization not only limits itself to address the subject from an economic point of view but it is also a narrow approach as it reduces globalization to a merely quantitative fact.

Thus, globalization would just be a quantitatively higher degree of the transnationalization phenomenon known so far by world economy, typified by worldwide expansion of transnational companies in industrialized countries. This expansion process enabled transnational companies to progressively turn the whole world into a great economic arena to place their subsidiaries, investments and products.

But we do not approach the phenomenon under study like that. The objective trend to interrelate the different world phenomena and processes—not only within the economy field but also to interrelate economy and other spheres of international life— has made it impossible to disregard multidisciplinary and multinational approaches when making a decision on many a contemporary matter.

Doubtlessly this multidisciplinary and multinational approach is very complex when trying to arrive at a settlement of the most rational solutions to certain situations in the economic, social, environmental and other fields.

The international context—characterized by the trend to political and ideological unipolarity, and the steps to-

8. Refer to A. de la Garza, "Globalización de la política," *Relaciones Internacionales* (México) 52 (1991), and Samir Amín, "El futuro de la polarización global, " *Realidad Económica* (México) 130 (1995).

wards a new world order undertaken by the main pow-ers—is not restricted to transformations in the current system of international politico-economical relations. A modification of the international institutional milieu is also pursued. In achieving this modification, not only new and very reactionary conceptions implying serious retrogression relative to the achievements gained so far through international law and cooperation relations are involved, but some modifications of international orga-nizations to sanction the ends pursued are also promoted.

The exaggerated relevance given to supranational mechanisms as being the most adequate way to solve global, national and regional problems may serve as an example for the above statement.

Thus the idea that it is convenient for certain coun-tries to yield part of their national sovereignty to a sort of "world governance or administration" which would make decisions on their behalf is beginning to circulate in certain international literature.[9]

These calls in favor of a "world or global administra-tion" do not seem to take into account the fact that we still live in a world marked by the existence of countries with very dissimilar development degrees, and that the so-called theory of interdependence—which stated that developed countries were supposed to be dependent on the underdeveloped ones—was long ago forgotten.

A "world or global administration" while there are na-tions with dissimilar trade capabilities and a world prone to politico-ideological unipolarity is a serious danger for underdeveloped countries.

Following the statement above, we are on the verge of a pseudohomogenization of the countries. The world

9. On this respect the following works may be referred to: PNUD, *Informe de desarrollo humano, 1992* (Bogotá: Tercer Mundo Editores, 1992), and Commission on Global Governance, *Our Global Neigh-bourhood* (Geneva, 1993).

is approaching this state of affairs by putting aside the special considerations contemplated to deal with less developed countries, and it happens precisely at a historical moment marked by the formation of great economic-commercial blocks and the deepening of the economic gap between North and South.[10]

It is also appreciated the push given to the idea that there is co-responsibility among all nations for the emergence and solution of global problems. Such a notion distorts reality and masks the relative degree of blame of diverse groups of nations.

This false egalitarianism that would be established among nations having very dissimilar development levels shall only bring about an increase of the international commitments of underdeveloped countries and a complete oblivion of the commitments contracted by industrialized nations to contribute to the socioeconomic development of the former.

Even though the transit from internationalization to transnationalization meant a reduction in the number of agents capable of influencing the designs, behavior and control of the international system of politico-economic relations at a given time, the globalization trend suggests a new decrease in the number of such agents and consequently growing segregation of the number of countries and people whose destinies would be at the mercy of a minority.

The *internationalization-transnationalization-globalization* sequence must be considered one of the poles along the development of the general law of capital accumulation enunciated last century by Karl Marx, but according to the contemporary international point of view.[11]

Since the origins of capitalism, colonized territories—which involuntarily helped develop the system in

10. Refer to H. Zamerman, "Sobre bloqueo histórico y utopía en América Latina," *Problemas del Desarrollo* (México) 95 (Oct.-Dec. 1993).

11. Vidal Villa, op. cit.

the "centers"—were continuously exploited as a whole. It made it impossible for them to escape from their subordinated position within capitalist world economy.

The evolvement of capitalism from one stage to the next did not generate substantial changes in the economic fate of our countries. These changes only seem to be rearrangements in the position of the countries—or reduced number of countries—that managed to step out of the raw-material exporting group and fall into the countries exporting finished or half-finished products.

Nonetheless, within the underdeveloped world both groups of nations could not essentially break away from the capitalist-system logic that assigned the role of being exploited by developed countries.

If at the beginning of capitalism development, exploitation adopted the form of plundering natural and human resources—Africans were forcefully taken away from their homelands and turned into slaves—, then it turned to exploit through the differences in economic structures, technological development, productivity level and import-export prices. Later on, capitalism created a wide spectrum of mechanisms to exploit our countries. Thus resource drainage would appear associated to the remittance of profits from foreign investments and, later on, high disbursements related to the potential use of modern technologies—which became a "special merchandise" and relevant export product by the developed capitalist countries—and those derived from the payment of the foreign-debt service.

The exploitation of underdeveloped countries seems to have followed two trends. On the one hand, there are the nations that suffered from a systematic exploitation by the present-day capitalist developed countries without having the chance to revert—even for short terms—that historic trend or being able to take advantage of eventually favorable politico-economic opportunities. On the other hand, there are the countries that, due to certain interests of the above-mentioned powers, received choice treatment under their very underdeveloped state. This fact enabled them to reach some degree of development which is expressed through some industrial installations, a rather-diversified economic structure, and certain degree of participation in world markets.

Although globalization is an objective trend derived from the evolution mentioned above' it is not a completely "natural" process as its present stage of evolvement is, now more than ever, being spurred on by forces giving globalization a particular character.

It must be remarked that there is a current attempt to give first-rank importance to the global problems industrialized nations are interested in, while those of underdeveloped countries—which happen to group up the majority of world population—are "forgotten" or second-rated.

It draws the attention the support offered by the main principal industrialized nations to the United Nations Conference on Environment and Development, and their efforts to reach a number of agreements on diverse environmental issues, while crucial problems like the foreign debt and the promotion of sustainable economic recovery are not yet solved—to say nothing of older agreements; for instance, the one referred to contributing with 0.7% of the GNP to the Development Fund.

The general law of capitalist accumulation is a process causing the displacement of people from the community of the employed to the army of the unemployed ones. At national scale, its structural and irreversible nature has originated segregation and underground economy. At international level such law likewise is generating the *segregation* of underdeveloped countries or groups of them which—due to their little economic and technical-scientific degree of development, their being producers of goods whose demand is stagnant or prone to decline, their facing up important monetary-financial problems, and so on—have been somewhat "forgotten" by capitalist developed states and major transnational banks alike. Segregated countries find in international donations from developed countries, multilateral organizations and nongovernmental ones (NGOs), their way to survival.[12]

The segregation of underdeveloped countries is not only a negative sequel of the globalization logic but also reveals the other face of its "rationality" which may even get to neither using the natural and human resources of some countries allowing those resources to be fully used for they do not serve the international strategies of the centers of world power.[13]

If the phenomenon of segregation—that all along the 1980s could be appreciated through the attitude of both imperialist countries and transnational companies towards the serious problems in sub-Saharan Africa (drought and extreme poverty) and Latin America (foreign debt and recessive economic adjustments)—indicates that the ruling circles of capitalist developed countries somehow do not care about underdeveloped ones, it seems that the consequences of globalization—which are beginning to shape up in the horizon of international politico-economic relations—will be more serious.

The segregation now threatening our countries will not be restricted to small little-developed or technologically backward countries that cannot play an important role in the international arena, i.e., segregation will not just be excluding a number of these countries because of their scarce economic and technical-scientific possibilities.

12. Samir Amín, op. cit.
13. L. Bendesky, "La dimensión del proceso de globalización económica," *Problemas del Desarrollo* 95 (Oct.-Dec. 1993).

Segregation could thus be defined as the superior degree of exploitation of our countries. It not only means our countries will be pushed aside because of exclusively economic criteria—for they are of no consequence regarding the economic, commercial, financial, and technical-scientific trends of the world to be—but also that their supposed nullity as economic entities would seem to approve their being treated as political nullities.[14]

Reconsidering Development-Underdevelopment Relation?

The basic principles that guided the efforts towards economic development up to the late 1970s have sneaked into the objective conditions generated by globalization. It then becomes necessary to reconsider what does development means and consequently, what relation may be established between this concept and its contrary—underdevelopment.

"Development" was launched as an official concept after World War II in the following context: international-system rearrangement, independence of a great number of former colonies, and growing ideological opposition between capitalism and socialism. The sequel of the colonial experience in most underdeveloped countries and the strategic-military and ideological bipolarism were the two main factors affecting North-South problems for almost half a century.

The end of World War II was a turning point in North-South relations as far as both activity and expecta-

14. Refer to G. González, "Notas sobre la geopolítica y el nacionalismo," *Relaciones Internacionales* 52 (1991), and S. Raymond, "La desaparición del Tercer Mundo," *Reforma Económica Hoy* 4 (1994).

tions are concerned. After nazism defeat, a prosperity period economically and politically led by the United States opened. The United States became the center of world capitalist development and erected itself the moral, intellectual and material leader of the system, in charge of reconstructing war-destroyed Europe while being bound to solve all international problems.

President Harry Truman used the term "underdevelopment" for the first time on his inauguration speech in January 1949 while referring to poor and backward areas of the world which on postwar conditions could—thanks to the technological miracle—come out of such a state of affairs. The statement derived from the idea that "all developed countries had at one time been underdeveloped ones, so today's developing countries will be the developed countries of the future."[15]

Viewed from the North standpoint, the North-South agenda consists of offering technical assistance, allowing market access for basic products from the South, and doing its best to make friends as to assure the alliance of strategically situated countries. The true needs of underdeveloped economies are not taken into account, and security concerns prevail on granting economic assistance.

Viewed from the South standpoint, the North-South agenda shapes itself in a confrontational context. Protracted colonial exploitation helped nourish the idea that the development assistance was a debt the former metropolises had contracted with the territories they had ruled. Development was deemed a people's right, not a goal to attain. The failure of the actions undertaken to achieve development was considered an aftereffect of colonialism.

15. Luis Maira, "América Latina frente a los desafíos del nuevo sistema internacional," *Diálogo y Seguridad* (Caracas) 1 (Dec. 1994), 51.

During the 1950s, the legal basis of the United States that granted foreign assistance was the Law of Mutual Security. South Korea and Taiwan became important recipients of U.S. assistance. Western financing for constructing Aswân dam was removed once Egypt showed its being prone to accept Soviet military assistance.

The 1960s registered an intensification of the North-South debate. The United Nations proclaims it the Decade of Development, and the European Cooperation Organization becomes the Organization for Economic Cooperation and Development. In 1964, the creation of the United Nations Conference for Trade and Development (UNCTAD) left no margin to doubt that the South considered its status quo resulted from the prevailing economic structure. So, if the North controlled the economic agenda, it was then necessary for the South to keep a unified position in the political field. This leads to the foundation of the Group of the 77 (G-77).

The creation of the Movement of Non-Aligned Countries institutes a "Third-World" angle in global politics,[16] due to the objective and subjective conditions created by Cold War. This process allows the South to keep an independent position regarding the East-West division which, in its turn, was reflected by the search for a neither-capitalist-nor-socialist economic model. It leaned to plan economy with authoritarian strokes, which was considered specially suitable to the postcolonial state of most members.

The debate on development also reached the academic plane. In the last few years of the 1950s, U.S. economist and ideologist Walt Whitman Rostow writes a very valuable work to legitimate the model of capitalist

16. Boutros Boutros-Ghali, "A New Departure on Development," *Foreign Policy* 98 (Spring 1995), 44.

development. *The Stages of Economic Growth. A Non-Communist Manifesto*[17] is a book defending the theory that all societies must go through five growth stages: (1) traditional, (2) conditions prior to takeoff, (3) initial impulse, (4) onwards to maturity, and (5) era of high mass consumption. Nine years later Rostow publishes a second book on politics and stages of growth in which he states that overcoming underdevelopment is just a matter of time for "in all developing continents there are countries which have shown—to their own satisfaction—their being able to progress on a rather regular basis at a substantially higher rate than the demographic growth rate, and this growth can be translated into greater welfare the people is able to see and feel. Trusting that children will live better than their parents is more important than filling up the abstract and statistically-ambiguous void between rich and poor nations."[18]

The economic prosperity in some underdeveloped regions—Latin-America for instance—seemed to backup that theory. From 1950 to 1980 Latin-American growth rate was higher than that of the United States and the whole European countries. Such a fact strengthened the optimistic expectation that the existing gap between these regions and the developed powers was being shortened.[19] Growth rates of all underdeveloped countries fluctuated from 5% to 6% during the 1960s and 1970s.[20]

17. Walt Whitman Rostow, *The Stages of Economic Growth. A Non-Communist Manifesto* (Cambridge: Cambridge University Press, 1962).
18. Walt Whitman Rostow, *Política y etapas de crecimiento* (Barcelona: Dopesa, 1972) (English edition published in 1971).
19. Luis Maira, op. cit., 51.
20. Fidel Castro, *La crisis económica y social del mundo. Informe a la VII Cumbre de los Países No Alineados* (La Habana: Oficina de Publicaciones del Consejo de Estado, 1983), 14.

In the field of Marxist ideas, the current for research and interpretation of the underdevelopment phenomenon—called the Dependentists—led by André Gunder Frank stood out. Frank defined development as a polarizing force that creates wealth in the metropolis and poverty in its satellite countries.[21]

Likewise, the model developed by the USSR and the East European countries of the so-called real socialism did not represent a real alternative for the countries in the South, not only because of starting-point differences but also due to its high degree of immobility and bureaucracy.

In spite of their heterogeneous development degrees and politico-ideological standpoints, underdeveloped countries put in practice development strategies following generally self-sufficiency schemes which favored strong state control over economy, the protection and creation of domestic industry—oriented towards import substitution—and the participation in regional integration formulas.

During the 1970s, the North-South problem became more poignant. The two special sessions of United Nations General Assembly on development turned into oral battles. The call to create a new world economic order launched at a NAM Summit in Algiers 1973 and the paradoxical consequences of the actions undertaken by the Organization of Petroleum-Exporting Countries (OPEC) opened a space for South-South cooperation, though feeble and brief.

At the same time, some pressure groups in the North itself mobilized to warn of the dangers lurking over humanity should the differences between developed and

---

21. André Gunder Frank, "El desarrollo del subdesarrollo," *Cuadernos Anagrama* (Barcelona) (1971). The English original was published in the magazine *Monthly Review* 18 (4) (1966).

underdeveloped countries were to continue. In this respect, the Club of Rome's reports *Los límites del crecimiento*,[22] *La humanidad en la encrucijada*,[23] and *Reshaping the International Order*[24] stand out. These reports together with the one from the Bandt Commission in the late 1970s had little impact on the North standpoints relative to the South.

The decade of the 1980s starts in the midst of a profound crisis of the capitalist system represented by a sudden interest rate upturn and the collapse of world demand for primary exports. For underdeveloped countries it meant the so-called Foreign-Debt Crisis due to their being unable to generate enough earnings to pay the loans back.

The Foreign Debt Crisis is a milestone in the North--South problem. Firstly, it is a consequence of capitalist-economy evolvement towards transnationalization after World War II. Secondly, the already mentioned trends that presently characterize globalization started to manifest by creating a qualitatively new stage in the process of capitalist internationalization.

Since the 1970s foreign direct investments in the South started moving towards developed countries and emerging economies in Asia. It was then replaced by indirect investments (loans) caused by the avalanche of petrodollars in their quest for quick profitability. Those financial flows not only engendered the major indebtedness that turned the 1980s into the so-called Lost De-

22. Dorella Meadows et al., *Los límites del crecimiento. Informe al Club de Roma* (México: Fondo de Cultura Económica , 1981).
23. Mihailo Mesarovic and Eduard Pestel, *La humanidad en la encrucijada. Informe del Club de Roma* (México: Fondo de Cultura Económica, 1975).
24. Jan Tinbergen et al., *Reshaping the International Order. A Report to the Club of Rome* (New York: Dutton, 1976).

cade—as far as development is concerned—but also initiated new ways of North-over-South exploitation.

Paying foreign debt obligations not only closed underdeveloped countries' road to development but also placed the poorest sectors of their populations on the toughest conditions. Assuring private institutions to pay their dues of the foreign debt became International Monetary Fund's (IMF) new role in the international financial system a duty it formerly assumed only regarding its own loans. The pressures the IMF applied on underdeveloped countries made these put in force structural adjustment programs to stabilize the economies following neoliberal criteria such as (1) decreasing consumption rates is essential to allow capital investment on domestic production segments, and (2) exposure to international investment and trade competition increases production efficiency.

Consequently, South countries became net suppliers of financial resources for the North creating a structural dependence on such transfers.

Furthermore, IMF conditionings became an instrument of political control over indebted states which, badly in need of financing, had to reshape their economies to match neoliberal patterns, and to open up to the free flow of transnational capital without any protection.

In the 1990s, monetary offers to developing countries are a consequence of world capital market globalization and deregulation of financial services enabling their great mobility' especially regarding bonuses and shares. Monetary offers do not respond to bank loans for production-related investments, but are mainly short-term allocations, potential-investment needs, and so on. Those are money sums mainly moving in the speculative sphere without any real impact on economy.[25] Save certain instances like the recently industrialized Asian countries, it seems globalization trends are extremely negative to underdeveloped nations regarding not only their aspirations to force underdevelopment itself but also, in a much wider sense, the very survival of those countries as sovereign and independent states.

Some implications of globalization relative to underdeveloped countries and North-South relations will be pointed out:

1. Capitalism has predominated all along the present century. In terms of development—although uneven—it has been prone to become a centrifugal force displacing tough productions activities towards countries with low-waged labor force in the periphery. This fact brought about an international division of labor whose consequences for development were similar to those capitalism caused in the 19th century regarding natural resource ownership—dual economies in which the foreign sector was not fully integrated, and the interdependence was asymmetrical. However, this international division of labor seemed to link North-South economies inexorably.

On globalization conditions, due to the companies' need to become networks— and paradoxically because of communication developments—, physical nearness gains vital importance. This fact has a centripetal effect on economic development; i.e., only South economies being able to offer the best educational and communication infrastructures to foreign firms while being situated geographically near the industrial heart of the Triad will be connected to the economies in the North.[26]

25. Berenice P. Ramírez López, "América Latina frente al proceso de globalización: retos y potencialidades," *Problemas del Desarrollo* 24 (95) (Oct.-Dec. 1993), 87-109.
26. Dunning, op. cit., 23.

The poorest countries would be even more segregated and would only benefit from the subcontracting of some activities requiring a lot of physical work.

2. Production immateriality—caused not only by automation, component miniaturization, and plant-size reduction but also by both substitution of natural raw-materials for man-made ones and service sector growth—drives capitalist economy off traditional companies. By extension, capitalist economy displaces itself from countries and regions producing material resources to those related to new activities. On such conditions, sheer industrialization—formerly an irrefutable sign of development to South countries—becomes an unattainable and unfeasible goal, and underdeveloped economies tend to increased segregation.

3. Regional integration to globalization lies in new bases, regarding the leadership of transnational companies in the Triad countries that are the "flagships"[27] of company networks. Integrating schemes imply North-South formulas—North American Treaty of Free Trade, North American Free Trade Agreement—that most countries are excluded from. Only the countries showing more powerful economies—once profound institutional reforms were carried out' and economic policies complying with North-imposed conditions were put in force—are allowed to join in.

South-South integration—as it has been essayed with little success in Latin America for some decades—would be limited to signing commercial agreements based on primary export specialization while abandoning old integrating concepts basically oriented to strengthen standpoints in bilateral negotiations with the capitalist power representing the integrating pole.

27. Ibid., 24.

4. World economic-power concentration and centralization in a reduced number of countries showing the most important mechanisms—those of financial capital—allow the North to force its political decisions upon the South—deprived not only of the USSR and the socialist camp as counterbalancing force in the international system but also of viable alternatives pertaining to a globalized market. Although the political offensive from the North is based on the objective processes of an economic globalization, it transcends them. The intention of imposing on the South cultural patterns reminding somehow European "civilizing mission" as ideological justification for colonial expansion can be seen through that move.

Beyond the necessary homologation of macro-economic policies according to the postulates of neoliberalism—which enables a free flow of capital, merchandise and services—, whose attainment involves all sort of pressures and conditions, the North tries to set its canons of political organization as additional means to control South countries whether in the field of bilateral relations or through multilateral formulas; i.e., by proclaiming that the features of the so-called Western political culture are universal values while dogmatically ignoring the various differences that make such a political culture impossible to be applied to other societies.

The neoliberal political agenda and the actions generated from the centers are aimed at establishing mechanisms in the international system which make sure the South states behave according to the rules outlined. To make that happen, the principles—sovereignty, self-determination, non-meddling in foreign affairs, and so on—international relations should be adhered to are discredited in the name of modernity.

To attain that goal, a number of concepts—democracy, human rights, and others—are used and exert a convincing intent because they are supposed to have a "refraining" effect on state powers, which may be considered to hamper national prosperity and international peace under the assumption that democratic, liberal states are less prone to foreign aggression as opposed to authotitarian ones.

The political offensive also works within underdeveloped societies. There it tries to identify which sectors and class strata of the population may be turned into both advocates of the globalization-intended values and impugners within the civil society.

The control that information and culture transnational companies exerts on mass media and the entertainment industry paves the way for creating groups that formulate opinions within particular societies, and shaping public opinion on certain subjects. That is a consequence of the weakness of education system in most underdeveloped countries, and the fact that the majority of their intellectuals studies in central countries. There the intellectuals are permeated by and adopt ideas, customs and consumption patterns which have nothing to do with their national realities.

5. Economy transnationalization has aggravated a group of problems which, due to their extent and unaddressability by a single country, have been denominated "global problems." Narcotraffic, international terrorism, environmental pollution, and so on, are among them. These problems couple with situations mainly affecting underdeveloped countries and become real or potential threats to international community—among those threats are famine, extreme poverty, exponential population growth, migrations, epidemics, and national and interethnic conflicts.

While that set of problems—whose different origins can be traced back to the economic and sociopolitical conditions generated by the capitalist system in central countries and in the periphery—is seen by the North as a threat coming from the South and not as items that deserve an immediate solution for the fate of mankind.

"Refraining" such threat is one of the underlying reasons in a number of proposals from the central countries. In the last few years, these proposals have dealt with restructuring the United Nations and other regional multilateral forums like the Organization of American States (OAS) and the Organization on Security and Cooperation in Europe (Conference on Security and Cooperation in Europe until late 1994). The proposals mentioned stress on the need for those organizations to accept new roles in the international arena so they may take on supranational functions formerly under the jurisdiction of the different states.

In all cases, the use of economic sanctions, political pressure and military actions are relevant elements. Efforts aim at making them acceptable in spite of their openly interventionist character. It may be noticed the adoption of new international-law categories such as "limited sovereignty," "preventive diplomacy," "maintenance and construction of peace," "humanitarian intervention," "democracy restoring," and so forth.[28]

Simultaneously, it is attempted to put in force programs strengthening North political power in multilateral forums. Take for example the increase in the permanent members at United Nations Security Council when Germany and Japan were incorporated, Canada's participation in the inter-American system by joining OAS, and the creation of the Council of Economic Security which restrains the margin of action of the South in detriment

28. Refer to Boutros Boutros-Ghali, *Un programa para la paz* (Nueva York: Naciones Unidas, 1992).

of the Economic and Social Council consisting of fifty-four elected members.

These proposals essay formulas enabling to lay the bases for a sort of "world governance" through the United Nations. Such governance should match the present internationalization stage and the unprecedented challenges internationalization has meant especially for the South. It has been difficult for the North to attain its goal mainly due to lack of consensus, without forgetting structural and procedure obstacles. Such facts defer the chance for world governance to come true in the immediate future.

However, in the meetings held by the Group of Seven, transcendental decisions—the ones having direct impact on world economy—are being agreed upon. So South countries have been compelled to look for means and ways to channel their demands into that forum of developed powers.

In 1989 the Group of Fifteen (G-15) was founded. It consisted of countries representing diverse world regions. Its aim was to form a high-level political group devoting itself to the consultation and analysis of the international situation. It tried to become a mediator between those countries and the Group of Seven.

The so-called Group of Rio, currently integrated by the 14 most influential Latin-American countries—also aims at mediating between the region and the Group of Seven. For instance, at the Group of Seven's 1955 Summit held in Halifax, Nova Scotia, in June, a proposal for restructuring the international financial system was presented by the Group of Rio.

Summing up, the international system evolvement is expressed through those trials and errors to settle the political structures and mechanisms enabling to attain

world governability in compliance with the changes occurred and the conceptions of their alleged leaders.

Latest World Trends
—Their Theoretical and Conceptual
Context

During the 1990s, we witness the development of
world trends resulting from the globalization process. At
the same time, the formation of a new theoretical and
conceptual concept can be appreciated. By means of it,
the actions undertaken by central powers as to arrange
"their" post-Cold War world order are intended to be legiti-
mized and be granted credibility. The principles that used
to be involved in the underdevelopment-development debate are abandoned.

It is wrong to state that this theoretical and conceptual context—elaborated by the think-tanks of developed
nations—has been formed during or is a consequence of the
last few years. Firstly, the above-mentioned context has
been formed jointly with the need to answer all the questions and situations resulting from the changing conditions generated by the world trends—this being one of its
most interesting features. Secondly, we think this new
theoretical and conceptual context is not a consequence
of contemporary contingencies, although present-time
realities have contributed to shape. The conceptions involved in such a context could be appreciated in Western
nations' thought currents—at the beginning, in the form
of "opposition" limited to certain academic circles, pub-
lications or political parties; then, gaining greater freedom and credibility from the new international context.

Since the middle of the 1960s, we witness a crisis of
the old world order shaped between the last few years of
World War II and the beginning of postwar era. This crisis

did not solely manifest in international economic relations but it expanded to other spheres of world events and to the superstructure as well. Let us mention a few examples of the impact of the old-world-order crisis on a certain increase of very progressive economic conceptions—which made Western political circles urgently carry out a politico-ideological counteroffensive: (a) the need to establish a new international economic order; (b) the economic and other relations among the states should be based on certain correlation of duties and rights; (c) the need of countries with a lower relative development level to receive differential treatment and/or of underdeveloped countries to gain access to the developed nations' markets; (d) the imperative of gaining consciousness of the seriousness and multifaceted nature of the global problems affecting humanity; and (e) the questioning of the development models and styles practiced in developed countries and the need to modify them.

During the last few years of the 1970s and the beginning of the 1980s, the above-mentioned politico-ideological counteroffensive from Western nations began. It involved both concrete actions regarding international relations, and the spreading of all kinds of novel conceptions.

The crisis of (neo-) Keynesianism-related expansionist policies and pressure groups associated with it, promoted neoliberal economic policies—whose character was completely opposite—connected to national and international conservative sectors. Due to different politico-economic contingencies, those sectors took over power in many important countries—like Great Britain and the United States—, and their conceptions gained worldwide acceptance. On the collapse of East European socialist regimes and then the U.S.S.R. dismembering, this status quo would further consolidate.

While in the 1975-1985 period—to set limits that are otherwise unaccurate—the politico-ideological counter-offensive of central countries had to face progressive conceptions elaborated in underdeveloped countries in the wake of the relevance acquired by the Movement of Non-Aligned Countries and the Group of Seventy Seven—although it was fading away at the time—, and those of socialist countries which still had certain degree of influence on international relations, after 1985 a steady progress of Western standpoints can be noticed. These standpoints did not solely involve interstate relations; their conceptions increasingly permeated the vocabulary and angles of the main international organizations—there included the United Nations.

The reasons behind this advance of new Western theoretical and conceptual ideas may be summed up as follows: (a) the collapse of the socialist camp which brought about serious questioning of Marxist-Leninist postulates, and the withdrawal of many leftist and progressive groups all around the world; (b) the reversal of the correlation of international politico-economical forces, and their unfavorable impact on the trading capacity of underdeveloped countries; it also meant that the standpoint-radicalization process in progress within these countries from the 1960s to early 1970s, not only stopped, but even fell back; and (c) leftist and progressive think-tanks were neither capable of making a quick and profound evaluation of the changes that were taking place in international relations, nor of elaborating and spreading integral conceptions backing up the idea of a new international economic order and other similar ideas which could become alternative theoretical and conceptual systems.

The Western theoretical and conceptual context has reached its climax under the triumphalist euphoria associated with the alleged unquestionable victory of capitalist mode of production over the socialist one. In that regard, it should not be surprising that the most significant aspect of the new context is the promotion of neoliberal ideas—a neoliberalism adapted to world conditions in the last few years of the 20th century.

The new theoretical conceptions are (a) to explain the advantages of the unchecked progress of capitalist production relations; (b) to backup all the actions favoring the current globalization process (from the capitalist viewpoint); and (c) to demonstrate the convenience of allowing a wider and freer performance of market forces.

This last idea is extremely important not only for economic conceptions but also for the whole set of conceptions of the new Western theoretical and conceptual context. In this regard, the critique of the so-called state of general well-being—a benefic and paternalistic state—occupies a highly relevant position. Such a state is charged with all the imbalances, deficiencies, and the rest of the problems, capitalism has shown during the last few decades, which have hindered its further progress.

The new theoretical conceptions—amply covered in neoliberal doctrine—seek to avoid for the diverse states to be involved in the problems and situations that affected their activities during the 1950s and 1960s. At that time, the states devoted themselves to act like capitalist executives as to spur national economies and awaken private sector interest in investing. They also—to a certain extent—were concerned with employment, public health, housing, education, social security, and tried to maintain a stable sociopolitical environment.

While under strong economic expansion, the states managed to conciliate rather well the latent pressing interests within capitalist societies, an economic slow-down—and what was worse, a crisis—was enough to make executives' standpoints prevail upon the workers'. The trials to artificially expand the economies led to increased inflation, fiscal deficits, and other imbalances causing the failure of (neo-) Keynesian policies.

The new theoretical conceptions—in a very smart way—relieve the states of such worries, and pass them on to the individuals. These, by using their initiatives, abilities and capabilities, make their own economic destiny. The success of some and the defeat of many would not then be a consequence of the operating laws of the system, but of the individual performance within it.

In this regard, on favoring the free performance of market forces at all levels, those new conceptions introduce a fresh ethic both for individual and nation relations. Hence, due to the devastating effects of the capitalist system—known to all, but defectively recalled by some—and its being spurred by the new conditions it acts on, some authors call today's capitalism *wild capitalism*.

The new theoretical and conceptual context is characterized by a return to the *individual as a political subject*. This fact results from the distortion of the critiques of the most traditional conceptions about economic development through the introduction of a new approach according to which development is to be considered as a human being-centered process.

The referred-to context tries to show the individual as a rather abstract, isolated entity. Thus, the context intends to blur the idea of an individual integrating wider collectives—social, ethnic and religious groups; societies; world population— and, as such, shaping his actions to comply with his relations with other individuals.

47

Then, as a complement of (rather a precondition for) well-promoted economic freedom, the individuals are entitled to so that their objectives are attained, a notable branch of the prevailing Western conceptions relates to political freedom. It was concretely expressed by a campaign in favor of human-rights-and-fundamental-liberties respect launched in the mid-1970s. This branch of political freedom did not limit itself to the notion that civil and political rights had to be respected. Some years later the campaign would widen to involve other subjects like democracy.

Regarding civil and political individual rights, Western statements have caused a widespread debate for evaluations on whether or not some states respect those rights and this has generated strong international controversial debates. Perhaps the most significant question is that, for some time, Western political circles managed to enthrone—in public opinion all over the world—the criterion that the human rights to be respected were exclusively the civil and political ones. Nowadays it has been possible to introduce economic, social and cultural rights as well in the evaluation patterns. Such circles state either that economic, social and cultural rights are a state commitment pertaining to the collectivity, or that they are human rights whose relevance is lower than that of civil and political rights.

Although the pro-human rights respect campaign was originally launched by the United States and other Western powers as a pressure tool over despotic and dictatorial governments, it was later on realized the convenience of drawing it against socialist nations. The campaign was however more than a tool for the international politico-ideological debate. On this respect, it is not always clearly noticed the campaign in favor of human rights respect—meaning civil and political rights, the ones defended by the West—implies focusing on the national field. Among other things, this statement means that (*a*) it distorts attention off global and interstate problems; (*b*) the ground is settled to allow certain international organizations to monitor domestic events (disguised meddling); (*c*) it intends to impose a sole pattern of human rights to be respected, which clearly means the purpose to homogenize the political behavior of the states—following this course it might even pretend to establish indexes to measure the freedom degree enjoyed by the citizens of a given country—; (*d*) it tries to weaken state power and authority through a continuous control or supervision from civil society grouped up in a heterogeneous spectrum of nongovernmental social organizations, and the like. Civil society then becomes "atomized," distracted, in a "laudable" function which neglects other no less important functions, but belonging to other levels of analysis.

The insistence on respecting human rights and the rest of the political liberties has swerved its emphasis. Now it tries to demonstrate this action is the foundation of a free act of the individual as an economic subject. The new conceptions are not only typified by a return to the individual as a political subject, but also by a return to *the individual as an economic one*.

While all the attempts made by Western countries' political circles and their ideologists as to hyperbolize the relevance of human rights and individual liberty respect, are an outrageous fraud—because, in truth, civil and political rights are promoted, while full self-fulfillment demands other equally important rights to be taken care of—, spreading the idea that conditions should be created for the individual to act freely on economy, is an even greater fraud.

The statement above is due to the simple fact that the possibilities for the individual to act freely on the economy are null on contemporary capitalist conditions. This capitalism is distinguished by huge transnational companies and banks which become an influence on the behavior of whole nations as a consequence of their economic power.

The return to the individual as an economic subject—likewise for the individual as a political subject—has various objectives within the latest theoretical and conceptual system of some circles in industrialized nations. Firstly, by raising the relevance of the individual with that double character, state authority and capability are reduced—this is part of the most modern thesis and actions of neoliberalism. Secondly, a link between the individual right to act upon politics and economy, and the ideas on the need to decentralize decision making is established; i.e., it pretends to show that the individual is capable of acting politically and economically at any level.

Once World War II was over, both capitalist and socialist states carried out all sorts of functions and so played leading roles in their respective societies. In the former, postwar economic restoration activities, economy spurring, and implementing the so-called well-being policies explain that fact. In the latter, likewise economic restoration and building up an economic system based on state property and centralized planning account for the statement.

A few decades later, due to all kinds of problems, the state action—mainly on economic issues—began to be strongly questioned. While such questioning has been backed up by economic arguments—excessive state intervention on economy, inefficient fund allocation, paternalism, and so on—we consider the main reasons have not been explained. These lie in the fact the state is a certain type of politico-economic entity related to such notions as national boundaries, sovereignty and self-determination, these aspects being obstacles for globalization aims; and in its turn, globalization is the goal the main world centers and their transnational corporations have in mind.

Consequently, in the new theoretical and conceptual formulations, a change in the publicness-privateness correlation may be noticed. Privateness is considered to be better suited to help the formation of major economic-commercial blocks, the implementation of supranational mechanisms, and, in short, globalization.

Although in the new conceptions under study privateness remains flawless—it does not undergo any essential change—, we consider publicness introduces some very interesting proposals. In our opinion, together with the revival of the politico-economic character of the individual, it is pretended to turn some of the publicness over to the so-called civil society or, at least, over to subnational entities—as a part of a decentralizing process in state activities—in search of a better resource allocation and increased efficiency. Another part of the publicness could remain under state control—a new kind of state, a re-created state. A third part of the publicness would be turned over to supranational entities or mechanisms. These would be in charge of designing, orchestrating and controlling the implementation of the policies by means of which the main global problems are addressed.

In this way, the new Western theoretical conceptions are not really proposing a simple change in the relative importance of publicness and privateness within each country, but a new approach to the doings of the agents regarding each of those aspects at national and—above all—international level.

The relevance given by the new theoretical conceptions to the international publicness is also related to the restatement of global-problems priorities under way. While in the early 1970s—when Cold War, armament rush and the reports of the Club of Rome were in full swing—the academic and political circles addressed, first of all, war-peace problems and development issues, followed by environmental pollution, natural resource depletion, demographic growth, and others, nowadays we are witnessing a devaluation of development issues, an unheard-of increase in the relevance of environmental degradation, and the inclusion of narcotraffic and terrorism as major world problems.

This shift in global-problem priorities is a logic consequence of the changes occurred in both the international correlation of forces, and the politico-economic context, which have enable to disregard the potential graveness of some problems while overestimating others.

In the new conceptions of global problems, the global implication of the above-listed issues are emphasized. Moreover, a detailed analysis of their causes or the dissimilar negative impact of such problems on diverse regions of the world is not undertaken.

Such a restatement of global problems is not a random act—the relevance of the problems is either decreased or raised, according to their assessed potential impact on stability and governability of the system as a whole. And, in short, for a faster globalization.

Due to the relevance given to globalization attainment through listing the diverse global problems faced by humanity, it follows that another significant aspect of the new theoretical conceptions is the apology of supranational mechanisms and the need to convince worldwide public opinion that the states should give up part of their sovereignty for the sake of collective well-being.

Once the real existence of certain global problems to be solved, and the lack of distinction between their causes and their diverse relative impact on different regions of the world are joined together, it follows that all nations must identically help solve those problems. It is the basis for the thesis of *co-responsibility* among nations. This thesis demands an equal share of responsibility from all countries, but dissimilar shares of efforts from developed and underdeveloped countries on the solution of global problems. Thus, the new conceptions in vogue mean a clear disappearance of any sort of special consideration for underdeveloped countries in general—or for the most backward ones in particular.

It not only means that all countries are considered alike—at least to contribute to the solution of global problems—and special treatment for selected groups are discontinued, but also that adhesion to neoliberal economic theses—with their demand for optimum resource allocation and efficiency pursuit—seems to legitimize the recent upheaval of diverse kinds of conditionings imposed by industrialized countries on underdeveloped ones if the latter wish to be granted assistance.

In order to assure favorable conditions regarding worldwide stability and governability which help reach the goal of globalization, the issue of international publicness is backed up with other arguments. Besides the global problems referred-to above, worldwide stability and governability could be affected by the outburst of national and regional conflicts which might bring about serious international consequences. Because of that, in the above-mentioned context a dangerous theorization—oriented to justify foreign intervention in the internal affairs of certain countries to solve the special humanitarian and military situations—has been taking place.

However, even at peace times there are other forms of international meddling in domestic affairs. In that regard, the establishment of monitoring mechanisms for diverse national contingencies is being promoted by different international organizations, and even intergovernmental forums. International or supranational levels or organizations designated for such purposes would be in charge of those monitoring mechanisms. Ideas about government transparency and the need for governments to periodically report are encouraged, while it is pretended to introduce diverse indexes that are supposed to measure up the progresses made by the governments regarding economic and social issues.

World Trends
and North-South Relations

The current process of globalization is the main trend in our times. We consider it a sort of summing-up trend whose manifestations can be appreciated in diverse spheres of world dynamics.

The globalization process is so important that not only explains the origins of some world trends examined in the present chapter but also decisively influences their quantitative and qualitative aspects.

Contemporary times are characterized by their complexity resulting from the emergence and development of a great number of trends in different fields. Such trends make it difficult to predict the probable course of international relations.

Main Trends of Technical and Scientific Development in the Last Few Years of the 20th Century—Their Consequences

In the technical and scientific field, the world in the last two decades of the 20th century can be distinguished by the crisis of a techno-economic paradigm—seemingly ensuing a system of international political and economic relations—and its replacement by a new one.

The accelerated changes in international economy since the beginning of the 1980s occur within the context of a structural crisis of capitalism and have been driven by the major transnational companies in search of higher profits. This strategy to overcome the crisis is more intensive than extensive and tries to increase productivity through technical innovation and management optimization, higher company diversification, new productive activities, more concentration and centralization, and finally through decreasing and reorienting direct investment flows.[29]

Though it cannot be said that the mass production system has been displaced, a flexible approach is edging its way in. Such an approach has been made possible thanks to technological breakthroughs in the 1980s and 1990s. For instance, computer-aided design and component miniaturization enable the use of multipurpose equipment and machinery. This type of production called "post-Fordist"[30] is a dynamic system in constant evolvement because the emphasis is focused on production process innovation and the upgrading of the characteristics of the finished products themselves.

This new techno-economic paradigm consists of the set of the technical and scientific breakthroughs that some literature refer to as *Third Industrial Revolution*.

While the old paradigm corresponded to a certain stage of world economic development—particularly of the capitalist system—featuring the continuous search for the biggest possible profits based on extensive use of natural, human and energy resources, the new para-

---

29. Refer to José Zaragoza, "El papel de los servicios en la restructuración industrial," *Problemas del Desarrollo* 24 (95) (Oct.-Dec. 1993).

30. The term "Fordist" or "Fordism" as applied to mass production system represents a "chain production" which is typical of the U.S. automotive industry. The term is named after Henry Ford, a pioneer of this industry.

digm came into being in a world aware of the finitude of some resources and the high degree of deterioration the environment has come to. So, when the features of both paradigms are compared to one another, we face a new economic, social, and environmental situation which in its turn demands new technical and scientific solutions.

The present techno-economic paradigm distinguishes itself by certain features that can be summed up as follows: (*a*) great variety of breakthroughs and inventions in diverse fields of science and technology; (*b*) the breakthroughs and inventions—due to the many-sided character of their applications—have reached almost every single sphere of human activity, causing a profound revolution in them; and (*c*) a search is on for better adequacy between basic-needs satisfaction and environmental and nonrenewable natural resources, among others.

The diversity of breakthroughs and inventions the new techno-economic paradigm consists of, is responsible for its major significance. In this regard, it might be said that recent technical and scientific advances have caused a substantial development of productive forces; i.e., they have determined basic transformations of not only work objects and means, but also of work force itself.

In terms of work objects, modern technical and scientific advances have created new man-made elements which, together with the natural ones, widen the spectrum of suitable materials to elaborate consumer goods and to implement services to satisfy human needs.

Work means have been quantitatively and qualitatively improved through the invention of many tools and devices—or through the upgrading of existing ones—by engineers and technicians, and the incorporation of such tools and devices in production and services.

Finally, work force itself has increased its capabilities and abilities through the progresses achieved in the medico-sanitary, educational-and-training, and other fields.

The latest technical and scientific advances the new paradigm consists of may be grouped up into four main areas as follows: (a) the emergence and development of microelectronics, (b) the advances attained in biotechnology, (c) the creation of the so-called new materials, and (d) the appearance of new energy consumption patterns

Although it would be extremely difficult to say which element of the so-called Third Industrial Revolution is the most important one, some authors give microelectronics development a lot of credit due to its many-sided impact on the most diverse aspects of human life.

Microelectronics not only meant a revolution in the field of data processing, information transfer and communication evolvement, but also brought about a dramatic turn in production modes. Such turn would influence existing productive systems based on mass production. In the future, owing to the many possibilities opened by microelectronics, production becomes more flexible. It enables to pay more attention to consumers' specific needs. Furthermore, flexible automation allows to separate whole processes—or some of their stages—while keeping centralized control on the operations through computerization.

The rising costs of research and development, together with shorter product life, force companies to combine their activities via the creation of vertical intercompany cooperation schemes and integrated production "network." Moreover, companies are prone to get rid of the activities that are not directly related to their main competing items, and to focus on value-added productions. Those two factors are increasing company dependence on outsourcing.

Thus, the production process of some manufacturing branches is being carried out in different locations which, to a certain extent, determines the current boom of intraindustrial and intracompany trade. Both trade modalities are typical of industrialized countries. It is estimated that the rate of intraindustrial trade reached 60% of worldwide trade in the mid-1980s, while intracompany trade represented 40% of it in 1990.[31]

At the same time, microelectronics enables to develop a greater variety of new products with an increased spectrum of specifications. Thus, the industrial application of microelectronics turns into a weapon for industrialized countries to introduce a quantum leap in the parameters to meet in order to have a competitive edge in the new market opportunities. The struggle for such market opportunities is on among the centers themselves.

From its information angle, microelectronics contributed to revolutionize the conventional notions of time and space. Hence, it has become an element of the present globalization process one cannot do without. That is especially true for economy. By means of fast data processing and speedy transmission of huge volumes of information, big transnational corporations are able to execute their profit-maximizing strategies in a better way, to allocate resources more efficiently, and to make more rational decisions as to develop production processes. At the same time—for better or for worse—microelectronics has aided the globalization of international financial markets as a consequence of its interconnection capabilities.

The development of computerization and telecommunications made it possible to run a global financial system. It allows national markets all over the world to

31. Ramírez López, op. cit., 97-109.

operate as if they were in the same area in spite of their being physically apart.

In other no less important aspects, microelectronics has meant a revolution and has made its contribution to the globalization process. By enabling the development of all sorts of communications, microelectronics has impressed managerial methods, and influenced education systems and even the way people enjoy their leisure time nowadays. In this regard, the technical and scientific basis of the longed-for model-and-style homogenization world powers pursue can be appreciated in microelectronics.

As to biotechnology, the forecast of its world impact —especially upon underdeveloped nations —can only be a very guarded one because of the unpredictable consequences, the very diverse courses biotechnological breakthroughs might have. Nevertheless, it can be already said that if microelectronics advances have been invaluable and revolutionary, biotechnological ones may turn out to be similar or even superior.

In former technical and scientific paradigms of the capitalist mode of production, it was evident a certain disequilibrium between the development degree reached by agricultural and livestock production and the manufacture industry for the latter had been consciously or unconsciously privileged.

The new paradigm in progress is seemingly characterized by introducing changes that—for the first time in history—could be translated into a simultaneous development of all the spheres of economy and, consequently, into the achievement of more harmonic economic structures.

From the economic angle, the possibilities biotechnology has opened for industrialized nations—which not only control by far the breakthroughs, but can also apply them on an industrial basis—could involve very adverse consequences for underdeveloped nations. The ability to achieve pest-resistant high-yield crops on inadequate sites and the possibility to breed optimum-quality animals, seem to be designed to deprive underdeveloped countries of their last sources of relative advantages and of their main export lines for world markets.

However, the most valuable thing about the advances introduced by biotechnology is that agricultural production could stop being dependent on natural factors—soil, seed and breed quality, rain and temperature profiles, and so on—which are so concerning for that segment of the economy.

Something similar is true for the third element of the new paradigm. New materials have meant an undoubted progress for humanity, and their appearance has substantial economic implications. Through the development and industrial use of new materials, the major powers solve a number of problems present in the old paradigm as follows: (a) the possibility of disregarding the eventual depletion of the sources of certain metals, minerals and other expendables; (b) to obtain expendables whose specifications are more uniform and so achieve higher-quality finished-products; (c) consequently, potential increased efficiency; (d) to obtain suitable expendable inputs for manufacturing extremely consumer-friendly items; (e) reducing—if not eliminating—expendables-availability dependence which avoids the danger of a supply crisis, for instance the so-called raw material crisis or the energy crisis at the beginning of the 1970s, and consequently attains a higher degree of stability and protection for the great world powers; and (f) to address the environmental pollution problem resulting from prevailing production patterns, among others.

New materials, jointly with microelectronics and biotechnology progresses, are dramatically revolutionizing, the bases for international competitiveness and national insertion in world economy. In the past, market advantages were sought through cheap and plentiful natural resources and work force, and maybe through the slowly-moving and much less monopolized technical and scientific progress; i.e., in many cases competitiveness chances depended on nature and the geographic situation of a given country—passive competitiveness advantages. Unlike the old market advantages based on competitiveness among nations and their place in the international division of labor, the current competitive advantages are consciously sought by men—dynamic competitive advantages. They are taking place so quickly that it is impossible for underdeveloped nations to maintain their positions within world economy. Consequently, save very few exceptions—a very reduced number of countries in Southeast Asia—, the common trend is for a decreasing participation of the underdeveloped world in global production and trade.

Finally, the fourth factor in the latent technical and scientific breakthroughs—the new energy paradigm—deals with and tries to solve another important deficiency of the former development patterns.

Regarding energy, current trends aim at a development in the following directions: (a) to look for less energy-intensive and/or more energy-efficient technologies and productive systems; (b) to develop and to introduce new energy sources and renewable energy sources not only to diversify the available ones, but also to avail humanity of undepletable sources of energy; and (c) to render compatible economic efficiency, production output, productivity levels, and environmental protection compatible in contemporary societies.

The progresses made by industrialized nations on the energy angle of the new paradigm will undoubtedly bring about a further decrease in the relevance of a group of underdeveloped petroleum-exporting countries, and the eventual—though remote—possibility of impacting the industrialized nations with actions like the petroleum shocks of the 1970s. Anyway, as the hydrocarbon (petroleum) is still the main—and sometimes the only—export product of those underdeveloped countries, decreasing world trends on demand and/or prices will surely and very negatively influence their economic fate.

A general balance of the latest technical and scientific progress seems to indicate that their diverse elements allow industrialized nations to attain a rather significant degree of independence concerning their supplies and other influences from underdeveloped nations. On the contrary, the new breakthroughs will cause not a conjunctional but a sustained reversal of the underdeveloped nations within world economy. Such a retrogression will increase their loss of negotiating capacity, and their being prone to undertake individual or uncoordinated actions. In the end, it will mean an economic differentiation that the central powers and their transnational corporations will take advantage of to put into force policies promoting selective relations.

Besides the already mentioned consequences—increased production output, increased labor productivity, globalization promotion, increased neglect of the underdeveloped countries by the developed ones, and so on— the new technical and scientific paradigm involves implications as relevant as the ones discussed below.

At first glance, the new technical and scientific advances have a contradictory consequence. On the one hand, they help stress capital concentration and centralization by transnational corporations because only they may be abreast of the research-development-investment-industrial application rhythm demanded by the new inventions and breakthroughs. But just because of that and due to the above referred-to technology features, the concentration and centralization of the capital relate to property, decision making, and global strategy planning, but it is not economically optimum to do it in terms of production because different technological and scaling problems must be taken into account. It is advisable to expand the installations up to a certain level and then start subcontracting parts and pieces from small- and medium-sized companies.

Therefore the globalization-oriented world might open some market niches for small companies, which would be linked to the great international production chain of transnational corporations, as these would help the small companies to outsource certain activities which could otherwise be either cumbersome or very costly to big world firms.

In keeping with that—and considering other impacts requiring further study— the new technical and scientific paradigm will bring about structural modifications in labor markets. The more the paradigm promotes remarkable transformations of the production structure, i.e., economy organization and management, the more the structure of necessary jobs will be transformed. As the new technical and scientific paradigm is imposing a knowledge-intensive economy, labor markets will be characterized by an increased demand of (highly) qualified work force in detriment of the unqualified one.

These changes in the labor markets will follow two trends. On the one hand, many emigrant workers from underdeveloped countries could face a "cul-de-sac situation." They had been so far absorbed in a certain degree by nonqualified and worst remunerated positions in industrialized nations. But developed economies are presently growing at very slow rates, so their capacity for absorbing work force has been sensibly decreased as new technologies showed their work force-saving capabilities since the beginning. This fact, together with the qualification issue, will undoubtedly affect South emigrants going North.

On the other hand, the new demands of the labor markets in developed nations will cause great tensions which will make governments and executives alike undertake work force requalification as number-one priority. The costs involved in requalification and education system redesign should not be considered as unproductive expenditures but as necessary expenses to assure production continuity and to use modern technology efficiently.

The new technical and scientific paradigm includes an aspect that is not new but does have new connotations. Being science and technology the most important elements of the production forces, these have turned out to be increasingly monopolized by transnational corporations, even more by the corporations that bear the heavy burden of research and development costs and employ most of the technical and scientific personnel in the world.

According to UNIDO data, industrialized nations laid out 95% of the research and development costs late last decade. Most of the patents were registered in those countries. These employ 90% of the technical and scientific personnel over the world.

Since the beginning of the 1980s a seemingly contradictory behavior in the industrialized nations—mainly in the United States—was appreciated. On the one hand, free trade is at all cost supported as part of the strategies imposed by the International Monetary Fund (IMF) and the World Bank (WB) upon underdeveloped countries.

However, the measures were intended to open up the way for the globalizing actions of transnational corporations rather than to attain free trade in the world—free trade that was and is still restricted by non-tariff barriers enforced by industrialized nations. These barriers are not yet subject to international negotiation. Thus, while that is the true state of the free-trade matter, in the field of intellectual property—both industrial and authorial—the industrialized nations strengthened their claims to obtain new international more-restricting juridical ambits to avoid unauthorized copies and usage.

The unquestionable importance of modern technologies coincides with the role of international trade as driving force for world economy. The central powers require for the trade dynamism to keep itself alive so it tows a slow-growth-prone productive activity. But, in order to assure such longed-for dynamism in the international trade, increased supply, new-product development, and new commercial bonds are required. The central powers consider all the above is achievable by monopolizing the technologies involved in the process.

Likewise they consider that in order to attain such a goal the elaboration of tougher national and international juridical standards on intellectual property observance are vital. Because of the close relation established among state-of-the-art technologies, new products and services, and their export to world markets, the great powers introduced the notion of the intimate links between trade and intellectual property rights. In keeping with this, they took advantage of the Round of Multilateral Commercial Negotiations in the General Agreement on Tariffs and Trade (GATT), held in Uruguay, to address this subject as a question of outmost importance.

In truth, the acknowledgement of the enormous political and economic importance of the intellectual property rights hid behind all that. These were used as both a domination tool and a means to obtain substantial incomes through license granting on patents and know-how.

Thus technical and scientific progress evolved from humanity heritage to special commodity whose prices—like those of a few goods listed in certain economic literature—could reach disproportionate high levels.

This situation reflects a valuable modification of the essence of international production relations and the basis of world power; i.e., they are moving from the property of the means of production to that of state-of-the-art technical and scientific knowledge.

It is evident that both national governments and supranational institutions are facing a number of brand-new challenges brought into the scene by the set of trends conceptualized under the term "globalization." It not only changes what is produced, how it is produced and where it is produced—a process that is a techno-productive and socio-institutional transformation, given its impact on employment structure, work force origin, and so on—but it also means, above all, a new phase of organization of the state and the world system which has been state-centered so far.

Moving assets across frontiers, the need for increased cooperation between the public sector and the private one; the changing role of the state in economy; the growing preeminence of the local, the regional or the global in detriment of the national; and the activation of nongovernmental organizations are some of the challenges the globalization process poses to the governments in a general sense.

In spite of the fact that the existence of supranational institutions has not only been one of the promoting factors of globalization but also its forefront, the challenge is not smaller for them. The increase in competition and interdependence among governments, the existence of a global market and a global financial system, and the emergence of a number of problems beyond the effective jurisdiction of the states demand answers that the present multilateral organizations—primarily either economic or political—are not ready yet.

Due to the embryonic character of the processes involved and the evident accompanying "paradoxes," the assessment of the consequences globalization has in store for the economic and social development—understood as material growth and life-quality betterment—can be started. However, current trends seem to indicate that the economic order those processes are forming, instead of auguring a more homogeneous and less conflict-prone world—as stated in the politico-ideological discourse divulged from the centers—, is a source of instability and disequilibriums. These will mark the evolving system of international relations with certain specific characteristics.

Although the implications of globalization pass over the old North-South division as the magnitude of the transformations affects both developed and underdeveloped countries, it cannot be denied that global processes impinge on those contexts differently.

While globalization generates conditions for more interdependence and symmetry among societies in the North—which would mean a world shaped after their values and interests—, for most countries in the South—lacking financial resources, deeply indebted, and politically unstable—it means a threat to their sovereignty, territorial integrity, and capabilities for economic survival.

Doubtlessly there is a high degree of communicative, informative, and institutional interconnection among developed countries. This fact is more evident within the European Union, but can be extended to the United

States and Japan. Consequently the Commerce and Development Organization is rather homogeneous though there are fractures and divisions there.

The uneven distribution of wealth, technical and scientific development and life quality accentuates the differences and increases the fragmentations not only between industrialized nations and developing ones but also within the developed countries themselves. Highly socioeconomically-developed areas coexist with wide segregation in both the North and the South which will increase conflict and detachment.

Globalization trends on the whole, do not seem to favor economic development for the majority of South countries. On the contrary, they emphasize the traditional dependence-and-segregation conditions. In this sense, the new stage along the capitalist internationalization process would mean canceling the hopes of overcoming underdevelopment for a lot of countries which do not satisfy the prerequisites demanded by transnational capital.

Globalization and Current Trends in International Economic Relations

The latest international context features the fact that certain political relations may coexist with some economic relations, and there is an intimate feedback between each other kind.

As it was stated in the previous chapter, a first step toward defining the globalization process is considering it as a quantitatively and qualitatively superior stage of the worldwide internationalization processes in which transnational corporations play a leading role.

Since the beginning of the postwar period, transnational corporations became powerful international economic agents. Their dynamism influenced the expansion, deepness, and course of international relations.

The objectives and limits of the present work do not allow us to relate in detail how, at the beginning, those corporations were a significant driving force for international economic relations and then began to impact such spheres as political relations, labor markets, and technical and scientific development.

On making themselves be felt in fields other than the economic, transnational corporations must be considered remarkable agents in the globalization process in progress all over the world. Through both their old and new strategies they have been shaping up a global approach to economic problems. So it is not wild to state that it is just in the economic field where globalization has advanced the most.

The current strategies of transnational corporations are influencing the emergence of new international economic trends. Thus, due to the actions from the main world companies, a new economic distribution of the world is originating. It is not based on the obsolete criteria of being backed by an extensive territorial rear guard—territorial distribution, influence spheres, colonies, semicolonies, and dependent countries—but it lies in the economic relevance of countries, economic sectors, and even just firms in order to achieve the global economic aims desired. As it has been stated by diverse specialists, geopolitics leaves its place to geoeconomics.

Through fresh strategies and criteria to maximize benefits, transnational corporations are radically changing the world economic map. Their activities have enabled them to concentrate a huge economic, commercial, monetary-financial, and technical and scientific power which has brought about a remarkable intensification of worldwide competition, and also the appearance of new ways to carry it out, or to avoid its more damaging effects. In keeping with this, during the last few years we have witnessed how corporations in a given field make alliances to one another to split the markets and to eliminate the negative consequences commercial wars among them might cause.

Since the last decade, other important trend in the latest international economic relations is the widespread dissemination achieved by neoliberal economic policies. Neoliberalist boom should be considered as the result of two converging reasons. On the one hand, the obvious crisis of (neo-) Keynesian economic policy to dynamize capitalist economies in the late 1960s and the beginning of the 1970s; on the other hand, the international financial institutions imposed those policies upon underdeveloped countries in the 1980s.

The gradual dissemination of neoliberal economic policies and their accompanying conceptions were more than just a new trend in international economic relations for they have meant a rather dramatic turn in the way to spur national and international economy.

The changes appreciated in the economic policies put into force in the world may be listed as follows: (a) the search for economic expansion as a basic dynamizing criterion is replaced by the contraction of the monetary mass and the equilibrium of the macroeconomic aggregates, and (b) the state's active nature as both economic entity and creator of conditions for maintaining the economic activity is replaced by a kind of state that limits itself to create legal or infrastructural conditions for the expansion of private entrepreneurs, among others.

It should be noted that one of the features of this new world economic policy trend is its perfect accommodation to the needs of the great international capital. On supporting at any cost the free performance of market forces, economic openness, and other liberal conceptions of this kind, world economic policies create conditions for corporations to penetrate and to control the economies of the underdeveloped nations.

So, as we have stated elsewhere, neoliberal economic conceptions should not be mistaken for neoliberalism itself. They are only the economic angle of a much wider politico-ideological project which is the philosophical basis followed by the great transnational capital and the power circles in the main world centers.

Unlike (neo-) Keynesianism, which foments an active role for the state—such a role should in the long run help it strengthens—, neoliberal economic conceptions seek to strengthen private entrepreneurs and make the state retire from a leading role. Thus, the economic conceptions sponsored by the International Monetary Fund and the World Bank are after weakening the entity which resisted the globalizing strategy while raising private entrepreneurs—who have not necessarily been eager to procure national well-being—to a relevant place.

The international difusion of neoliberal economic policies through underdeveloped nations resulted from the possibility opened by the foreign indebtedness crisis. It enabled not only crediting developed countries and banks, but also international financial institutions to impose measures for the structural adjustment of indebted countries.

We consider that by implementing neoliberal economic policies almost all over the world the central powers could open a new stage called *collective neocolonialism* in some Marxist-Leninist literature. This term was conceived either to depict such situations in which a given colonial power was too weak to keep its colonies and so other colonial powers came to its rescue, or to refer to the typical agreements—like the Convention of Lomé—between developed nations and underdeveloped ones. However, nowadays collective neocolonialism adopts deeper and subtler ways by incorporating international organizations which make neocolonial actions seem highly legitimate.

As stated above, neoliberal economic policies developed when the main world powers had activated the homogenization-prone mechanisms. Nonetheless, putting aside differential measures to treat individual underdeveloped countries, and replacing them by a "general recipe" as far as economic policy is concerned, the ensuing effect is an even greater deepening of the differences between the diverse groups of underdeveloped countries, which hinders their unity, common acting and negotiating capacity in face of developed countries and the international organizations in their wake.

While the differential trends—in terms of economic behavior—had been forming as a consequence of diverse selective strategies and policies put into force by industrialized nations and their transnational corporations along the preceding decades, by the last decade of the 20th century, the features of some groups of underdeveloped nations are sharply outlined and their respective economic behaviors can be effortlessly discriminated.

One of the main consequences of neoliberal economic policies appreciated in many underdeveloped economies is that their application originated changes—generally negative ones—in economic structures. On making this nations adopt an open-door policy and remove subsidies to export-intended productions, the commercial policy of many underdeveloped nations—firstly—and their production structure—afterwards—suffered noxious impacts regarding their economic growth goals.

Manufactured products and other nontraditional products of underdeveloped countries for the export markets—countries which could only get to world markets aided by certain degree of state protection—had to back away. So, in order to get the necessary superavit in commercial balances to satisfy the obligations of the foreign debt, the underdeveloped countries had to increase production and export levels of their traditionally export products—generally basic products. That action had a regressive effect on both their productive structures and world market prices.

However, while that was happening in the underdeveloped world, the situation was quite different worldwide. The technical and scientific progress has caused a vigorous development of services in the industrialized nations. Such development has determined a substantial change in the economic structures of the world—mainly those of developed countries although it can also be appreciated in some underdeveloped nations—consisting of an increase in the GNP or GDP share contributed by the tertiary sector, and also a raising in the percentage of work force employed by this sector.

According to our opinion, that structural change is not a simple economic fact but one of the crucial manifestations of our times. It has been caused by the convergence of two trends associated to the development of world productive forces. On the one hand, a marked increase in service outsourcing is appreciated. Economic and technical reasons have prompted the foundation of specialized companies which offer services previously executed by personnel belonging to the centers of production themselves. On the other hand, the emergence of new types of services associated to the variety of technical and scientific improvements originated by the so-called Third Industrial Revolution. Such services as data processing, transportation, communications, finance, and consultory have established an intensive interrelation with the economic activities. They have influenced in one another's growth. Together, they have aided the globalization process.

The service sector—also called tertiary sector, and formerly referred to as an unproductive sector in economic literature—has not only revolutionized many aspects of the different spheres of economy but also it decisively influences other fields of human activity, for instance education and leisure.

The service boom has affected the strategies of diverse states, which have had to progressively adapt their economic structures to profit from the new developments. In this direction they have tried to maintain or to increase former competitiveness levels enjoyed by their export products, and so assure keeping a favorable position within the international division of labor. Besides, transnational corporations had to carry out a timely modification of their expansion strategies to make the most of this new and relevant action field. Should the latest actions of transnational corporations be reviewed, it can be noticed how they have slowly turned their operations toward the service sector.

There are two kinds of services: (a) traditional services characterized by such activities as commerce, transportation, tourism, and others of the sort employing generally a lot of work force with low qualification and productivity, and (b) modern services consisting of a new generation of services technically and scientifically developed by the latest breakthroughs which employs a highly-qualified work force whose demand is increasing steadily all over the world. It influences almost every field of human life.

Analyzing the economic structures of underdeveloped nations might lead to wrong conclusions for there a raise in the importance of the tertiary sector is appreciated. However, if a detailed study were made, it would show that in truth most underdeveloped countries concentrate service sector activity on the so-called traditional services as opposed to the trends in industrialized nations. Thus we would like to remark that there is a substantial structure disequilibrium between the underdeveloped countries and the developed ones. It has and will have highly adverse consequences for the former group.

One such serious consequence underdeveloped nations are suffering—which is another of the prevailing world economic trends—originates where the new expansion strategies of transnational corporations, the modalities adopted by the technical and scientific development, and the economic activity boom converge at. As a result of this peculiar convergence, the world is witnessing substantial transformations of the productive system as to make them match both new globalization demands and the need for continuous capital valuation.

Hence, the most outstanding manifestation of such modification is the progressive giving-up of mass production and its replacement by the so-called flexible production. This modification is not restricted to changes in manner and/or means of production realization. The transformations are a lot deeper as they spread over to the field of company organization and management, company location, its world ranking, and so on.

The joint action of the new transnational-corporation strategies, the latest technical and scientific breakthroughs, and the emergence of new service activities—or the modernization of the existing ones—not only translated into productive system modifications but also are decisively changing both the competitive conditions of the nations and their place within the international division of labor.

Although it seemed that the post-World War II period was likely to consolidate such an international division of labor that developed countries would specialize in manufactured productions and export while underdeveloped countries would specialize in basic products, the experience of the new industrialized countries in Southeast Asia and some Latin-American countries showed that certain regions of the underdeveloped world had factors enabling their production to be internationally competitive. As a reaction to that fact, some developed nations started to build up new-type protectionist barriers—nontariff barriers—to hinder exports of those underdeveloped nations into their markets.

However, in the recent past, technical and scientific development has introduced radically new conditions to assess the competitiveness degree of nations. It progressively depends on the technological development of productive processes, and so the most competitive products are those being knowledge-intensive. Past are the time when competitive productions depended on intensive employment of low-waged unqualified work force and/or plentiful natural resources.

Thus the possibilities for the underdeveloped world as a whole to be able to elaborate internationally competitive productions are decreasing. Only an exiguous number of underdeveloped countries seem to be achieving it while diverse economic and juridical conditions—among others—are further restricting the chances for the remaining underdeveloped countries.

Or to state it otherwise, while in the past the competitive conditions of the countries were related to static factors, nowadays they are based on dynamic factors because highly depend on technical and scientific development. However, as this technical and scientific development is very swift and—as it was discussed in other section of this work—highly monopolized by the world power centers, there are substantial reasons for underdeveloped countries to face a lot of difficulties not only when trying to achieve adequate flexibility in their productive processes but also when attempting to keep these processes at internationally competitive levels.

The above-mentioned changes in the conditions of the productive system and international competitiveness in their turn influence the participation of the diverse countries in the international division of labor and their insertion in the world economy.

Contemporary world economic geography is distinguished by the emergence of new productive sectors and the decline of the former economic-growth "locomotives". Because of that and the rather fast ability shown by some countries or groups of countries to adapt themselves to the modifications taking place in the productive structure of the world, we are witnessing significant changes in the international division of labor and their insertion in the world economy.

Closely related to all the trends and other international economic phenomena so far examined, there is the formation of three great economic-commercial blocks headed by the United States, the European Union (particularly Germany), and Japan.

We consider that some of the features of the current international political and economic environment—for instance, the globalization process and the increased competition among the great world centers—seem to be the main causes for this novel tendency to form nation groupings whose nature fit between the 1930s blocks and the integrationist schemes which originated during the 1950s and the 1960s.

The new economic-commercial blocks take from their predecessors the idea of forming nation groupings spinning around a metropolis which they have economic, commercial, financial, and historical links with. But as the international economic, juridical, and institutional context is different, these new blocks are less prone to closeness or at least they are not as close as the blocks in the 1940s.

The blocks headed by the United States and the European Union are structuring themselves from an integrationist-agreement core. In the first case, it is the North-American Free Trade Agreement (NAFTA) which was put into force in January 1994. Its antecedent was a similar treaty signed between the United States and Canada. In the second case, it is the outcome of a long and progressively-deepening integrationist process. Finally, the Japan-headed block groups up neighboring nations without any economic or other kind of agreement. This fact shows that the formation of economic-commercial blocks does not follow a single pattern but adapts itself to specific economic, political, and geographical conditions.

Perhaps the most valuable aspect in the formation process of economic-commercial blocks is beyond the economic sphere itself. The process shows a contradiction between the globalization trend—interpreted by some political circles as the standardization or homogenization of the world, i.e., believing in the possibility for a single world power to stand out—and certain dispersion of the economic, commercial, monetary-financial, and technical and scientific power among the three great power centers.

Hence a dichotomy is appreciated. While the United States still plays a leading role in the political and military spheres, there are two other power centers—to say nothing of some upcoming poles which, according to certain expert statements, might become world powers in the near future.

Such a division of the world in three blocks seems to be the best exponent of the real situation in the last years of the 20th century: We are living in a changing world. We are living in a world whose trends are multiple and many-sided. These trends are sometimes contradictory and so hinder a certain prediction. We are living in a world showing a definite proneness to polycentrism.

As far as international economic relations are concerned, one of the recent grave tendencies appreciated is the evident retrogression with regard to international cooperation links. This fact is especially true when it comes to underdeveloped countries. The most important manifestations of such retrogression are the stagnation—and even the reduction—of the financial resources granted as official development aid, and the increase in the number of conditions to be complied with by the potential recipients.

Many an argument can be gathered to explain the reason for the changes in the conceptions standing since World War II ended. An argument is the so-called "aid fatigue". It consists of the supposed tiredness of both tax-payers and aiding governments due to the evident slow progress made by underdeveloped countries in the matter of economic growth and social progress. Other argument—somehow related to the previous one —intends to clarify the fact by indicating that in the developed countries there is public resistance to keep on offering resources to be wasted or—at best—inefficiently used by underdeveloped-world governments. Another argument is the need for underdeveloped nations to see to many economic and social problems recently accumulated.

Regardless the credibility margin the reader may confer to each argument above, it seems suspicious such a reconsideration of the aid-for-development policy comes into being precisely at a time of neoliberal economic policies which request circulating-cash contraction, ending of subsidies, activation of market forces, and the like. They are the ferment for a turning point in presumably paternalistic attitudes from the states to the citizens, and from the multilateral organizations to the recipient countries.

It is also convenient to draw attention to a number of additional arguments that explicitly call to reconsidering the priorities in the resources granted as economic aid as to allocate them for countries fulfilling certain prerequisites. In other words, a extremely selective international cooperation policy is promoted. Such a policy aims at bending state standpoints, fomenting discord, and in short reducing the negotiating capacity of the underdeveloped world.

Some Considerations on the Most Recent Social Trends

The emergence and development of new trends in diverse social problems also characterize the last years of the present century. In our times the most dramatic and substantial social question—which will be our leitmotiv along the analysis of contemporary social trends—is *poverty*. As we shall try to explain further on, this matter is dramatic because poverty grows in absolute and relative terms in a world where huge productive, material, and technical and scientific possibilities have been developed in order to raise the living standards of the inhabitants of the planet. And it is important because statistical yearbooks and studies on the question have shown the seriousness of such a phenomenon—a seriousness that may have unpredictable sociopolitical consequences.

We consider that a research on poverty and its many-sided consequences must start by clarifying the impact of two questions that are fundamental. The first one is the nature of world demographic trends; the second one is the evolution of economic growth, incomes, and the character of their distribution.

Most of the studies on demographic trends were deeply marked by the politico-ideological debate which opposed T. R. Malthus and K. Marx's respective viewpoints on the subject. Fresh, more rigorous and comprehensive approaches on demographic trends only appeared rather recently—around two decades ago. They are adapted to the prevailing conditions of world development. So since the beginning of the 1970s the demographic problem has become an important global issue regarding not only population growth in itself but also its many implications.

According to a study by the United Nation's Department of Economic and Social Development, world population reached 5,500 million people by mid-1992, and its annual average growth rate had come down to just 1.7% during the 1975-1990 period from 2.1% during 1965-1970. But those figures hide very uneven behaviors in developed and underdeveloped regions of the world. Due to the different annual average demographic growth rates (0.5% and 2.0% in 1985 and 1990 respectively), an increase in underdeveloped nations' population was appreciated. The growth was both in absolute and relative terms.[32]

While in 1950 world population relative proportions were 29.9% and 70.1% for developed and underdeveloped regions respectively, those in 1990 were 20.6% and 79.4%. The estimates for 2025 proportions might

32. All data on demographic trends were taken from ONU, *Informe acerca de la situación social del mundo, 1993* (New York: United Nations, 1993).

be 14.6% and 85.4% for developed and underdeveloped nations, respectively.

During the 1950-1955 period, population increase was 23% for developed regions and 77% for underdeveloped ones. Conversely, from 1985 to 1990 the relative percentages were 7% and 93% respectively.

Just as world population growth conceals the differences between the two main zones the planet can be split into, a similar situation may be found in the underdeveloped world. On reviewing the figures on demographic behavior in Asia, Africa, and Latin America from 1950 to 1990, three growth patterns are found: (a) Latin America follows a gradually decreasing rate (1950-1955, 2.7%; 1965-1970, 2.6%; and 1985-1990, 2.1%); (b) Asia follows a fluctuating pattern (1.9%, 2.4%, and 1.9%), and (c) Africa follows a clearly increasing trend (2.2%, 2.6%, and 3.0%).

Such an intense demographic growth in underdeveloped nations brought about a population density estimated as high as 541 people/1000 hectares compared to only 225/1000 hectares in industrialized countries. It also puts huge pressures on land and new job requirements. It is estimated that 6 million new jobs will be needed in the 1990s, and 10 million by the beginning of the next millennium.

Resulting from dissimilar population growth within the underdeveloped world, both the population and the relative proportion of the underdeveloped region in relation to world population (and that of the underdeveloped world) changed in the period under study. The relative participation of African population in world population grew from 8.8% in 1950 to 12.1% in 1990; in Latin America, from 6.6% to 8.5%; and in Asia, from 54.7% to 68.8%. According to estimates above, the population in Africa, Latin America, and Asia will represent 18.8%, 8.9%, and 57.7% respectively by 2025.

The behavior of world population in general—and of underdeveloped countries in particular—is the outcome of the interweaving of the trends followed by gross birth rate, fecundity rate, and death rate. The underdeveloped countries' gross birth ratio was 33:1000 in 1990 compared to a 15:1000 ratio in industrialized nations. Birth ratio however was as high as 45:1000 and 47:1000 in the most backward countries and sub-Saharan Africa, respectively. The world birth rate shows a decreasing trend. It came down to 3.45 births/woman in 1985-1990 from 3.60 births/woman in 1980-1985.

Nonetheless fecundity level in the world has been strongly influenced by its evolvement in underdeveloped countries—especially the most backward countries. Such evolution compensates the developed regions' achievements. While in 1985-1990 the fecundity rate was 1.9 in developed regions, it was 3.9 in underdeveloped nations.

An analysis of fecundity in each continent forming the underdeveloped world showed similar fecundity rates in Asia and Latin America (3.5 births/woman, and 3.6, respectively), while it was above 6.0 births/woman in Africa.

This tendency toward a slight fecundity-rate decrease in underdeveloped nations contrasts with the substantial death-rate decrease which consequently raises life expectancy. It is due to worldwide significant hygienic and sanitary advances and their diffusion through underdeveloped countries thanks to diverse campaigns led by international organizations, governments, and other entities. In those countries, death rate was estimated at 7:1000 in 1990.

In mid-1990 it was estimated that one out of three people in the world was a child, one out of five was more than 15 and less than 25 years old, and one out of 16 was 65 years old, or older. It means that approximately

40% of world population was 25-64 years old. By definition, the economically active population is that in the 15-64 year old range, so in 1990 the relation between the dependent population and the working population was 63% compared to 70% in 1980.

Once again world figures conceal the unfavorable situation of underdeveloped nations in terms of population structure. While in developed countries the 15-64 age group grew from 64.7% to 66.6% of the total in 1950-1990—which meant a dependency rate of 50% in the latter year (53% in 1980)—, in underdeveloped nations it changed from 54-59% to 51-62% over the same period. These percentages resulted in dependency rates between 61% in Latin America and 93% in Africa for an average of 77% for the underdeveloped world in 1990. So those figures indicate that while the dependency rate stayed almost constant in developed nations, the situation in underdeveloped ones worsened —whether they had initiated the so-called *demographic transition process*, or not.

Such a difference in the structural behavior of the population in developed and underdeveloped zones translated into considerable socioeconomic problems for the inhabitants of underdeveloped countries. In developed zones there was a tendency to a low rate in the 0-15 age group, and to a high rate in the 15-64 age group. However, in underdeveloped zones it was observed a tendency to a higher rate in the 0-15 age group than in the 15-64 one.

The previous statements can easily be verified by noting that, in 1990, 85% of the world population below 15 year old belonged to underdeveloped countries, and was estimated to reach 88% by 2025. Nonetheless the increase in longevity meant that 55% of the world population over 64 years old lived in underdeveloped countries back in 1990.

The negative impact of the demographic characteristics in underdeveloped countries is no restricted to its growth rate, density, or the peculiar relation between the dependent population and the economically active population. The international socioeconomic literature increasingly attracts attention to the *explosive urbanization process* in the underdeveloped world.

While, in 1975, 26% of the underdeveloped world population lived in urban areas, in 1990 it had grown to 37%—eight points below the world average. It is estimated that the urban population proportion in the underdeveloped world will be 45% (51% worldwide) by 2000 and will grow up to 61% (65% worldwide) by 2025. It shows how the urbanization rate will rise in underdeveloped countries. This is a consequence of the dramatic urbanization rate in these nations. It is estimated to reach 289% in 1990-2025 up from 92% in 1975-1990. Only in 1985-1990, urban-population growth rate was 4.5% in underdeveloped countries; it was almost six times higher than the developed countries' rate. Such urbane population growth rate was twice higher than the demographic growth rate in developed countries (2.1%) over the same period.[33]

Anyway, the average figures for the underdeveloped world disguise very uneven situations, such as the prevailing in the most backward countries where urbanization is about 20-30%; in Africa and Asia, 34%; and 72% in Latin America.

On analyzing the changes in the internal distribution of population in underdeveloped nations, some factors may be noticed, among them: (a) the critical situation of the agricultural and livestock sector due to obsolete land ownership and exploitation systems; (b) internal migrations caused by either objective expectations—job opportunities resulting from the development of manu-

33. Refer to ONU, op. cit.

facturing and service activities mainly in cities—, or subjective expectations—associated to the chances for higher living standards—; (c) natural disasters; and (d) armed conflicts.

Disorderly internal migrations in countries lacking a good infrastructure or the resources to create it rather quickly have contributed to the proliferation of marginal neighborhoods on the periphery of great cities with their sequel of low-productivity informal activities, and others whose social usefulness is dubious.

As a consequence of the magnetic effect of capitals and big cities on migrant population in underdeveloped countries, a paradoxical phenomenon can be appreciated: While in 1975 five cities of the underdeveloped world were among the ten biggest urban conglomerates in the world, in 1990 the figure has risen to seven—the outstanding fact being the most populous city belonged to the underdeveloped world: Mexico City, with its 20.2 million inhabitants.

A peculiar modality of internal migrations in underdeveloped countries is the so-called displaced people due to depleted soils, draught, and armed conflicts, among others.

The last aspect of demographic movements in underdeveloped nations worth mentioning is that of international migrations. Although in the international migration phenomenon political, economic, and social causes converge , it is also true that precisely during the so-called lost decade, the number of migrants to the main traditionally receptive world centers increased. Thus, some 3.5 million people migrated to the United States from 1985 to 1990, while there were some 13 million foreigners settled in the "Twelve"—countries forming the European Union until 1994—by the last years of the 1980s.[34] The virtual economic stagnation

34. Ibid.

widespread in the underdeveloped world encouraged big waves of people to look for employment and better living standards in the most developed countries.

The economic stagnation appreciated in developed countries in the first years of the 1990s, the rapid expansion of xenophobia, and armed conflicts, like the Persian Gulf War, have made emigrants return to their countries of origin with the ensuing socioeconomic adverse effects. The Persian Gulf War alone made 2.3 million people repatriate.

To assess the economic significance of emigrant workers, take for example that, according to an study made by the International Monetary Fund in thirty four countries during the last years of the 1980s; their money transfers represented 10-25% of hard-currency income in 15 countries, 25-50% in 8 countries, and more than 50% in one country.

A second factor conditioning poverty is economic growth. Underdeveloped countries grew 4.5% in 1988; 5.5% in 1989; 3.0% in 1990; 3.4% in 1991; 4.9% in 1992; 5.2% in 1993. The estimate for 1994 and the prediction for 1995 were a 5% growth.[35]

The economic growth rates in underdeveloped countries must be carefully studied as they may lead to false conclusions if superficially approached. Although underdeveloped nations show the highest economic growth indexes since the last years of the 1980s, such percentages conceal the fact that most underdeveloped-world economies are making an effort to recover from the ill effects of the "Lost Decade" resulting from entwining economic crisis, foreign-debt crisis, and enforcement of restrictive-type adjustment policies. It should also be noticed that the general development rate does not allow to distinguish the clear differing trends observed within the underdeveloped world. For

35. Refer to ONU, *Estudio económico y social del mundo, 1994* (Nueva York: United Nations, 1994).

this purpose it can be divided into three big groups: (a) zones with a high and steady growth (China, southern Asia, and the Far East); (b) zones with an increasing growth tendency especially since the beginning of the present decade (Middle East and Latin America); and (c) zones showing quasi-staganation or very small increases (Africa).

Other aspect to be taken into account is that a true assessment of economic growth in underdeveloped countries should lead us to study the gross domestic product (GDP) per capita as it is an index that helps a clearer evaluation of reality. Considering the demographic growth in the underdeveloped world can be three times and even four times higher than that of the developed nations, it may be understood its real economic chances are remarkably limited.

It should be added that the adjustment policies adopted by many underdeveloped countries have significantly increased the uneven income distribution not only between developed and underdeveloped countries but also within them. In the 1990 Report on Human Development elaborated by UNIDO it is stated that while in 1960 the richest 20% and the poorest 20% of world population obtained 70.2% and 2.4% of the incomes, respectively—a 30:1 ratio—; in 1989, the ratio had become 59:1. On the other hand, a study made by the World Bank showed that the poorest 20% of Latin-American population only got 4% of total while the richest 10% concentrated 60% of it. Finally the above-mentioned UNIDO's Report indicates that in Brazil the richest 20% get 26 times higher incomes than the poorest 20%.[36]

Although we have commented on the classical North-South income-distribution disparities, and also on the disparities within the South, the latest economic

36. PNUD, *Informe de desarrollo humano, 1990* (Bogotá: Tercer Mundo Editores, 1990), 86.

world trends are causing an unheard-of increase in income-distribution disparities within nations of the North where talks about "poverty bags" have started. So globalization dynamics has not only boosted the appearance of exclusion-prone mechanisms affecting whole (underdeveloped) nations but has also involved part of the industrialized countries' population.

Demographic and economic-growth trends for both the whole world and the underdeveloped world do not match each other. One of the main consequences of such a situation is the aggravation of the employment problem.

A report by the United Nations revealed that world work force was 2.4 billion people in 1990, of which 1.8 billion (75%) belonged to underdeveloped countries where the economically active population was 43.9% of the total population.[37]

To have a clearer idea of the structural disequilibrium we wish to examine, it would just be necessary to note that underdeveloped countries represented 82% of world work-force growth rate in the 1970s; 88% in the 1980s; and it is estimated at 92% in the 1990s. Nowadays some 38 million people are looking for employment annually in underdeveloped countries. Therefore it is considered that to be able to absorb such a volume of work force underdeveloped economies would have to show an average 6% annual growth rate in the 1990s. And to achieve this their net investment and gross investment rates would have to be around 24-27% and 32-34%, respectively.

The conditions prevailing last decade only allowed underdeveloped nations to reach figures nowhere in the neighborhood of those percentages, and so they could not absorb a significant proportion of people whose age

37. Naúm Minsburg and H.V. Valle, op. cit., 49-50.

make them apt to work. As a result of that, the amount of unemployed or underemployed people has increased. Regarding this last statement it must be said that the structural causes have become more relevant than the junctural ones. The latest world unemployment and underemployment data give an estimate of some 900 million people.[38]

However, those quantitative considerations are not the most important questions but the increasingly structural character of unemployment and underemployment which mainly in underdeveloped nations is generating the so-called *process of segregation* or *informalization of the economy*. According to such a process, some parts of underdeveloped nations are not fully incorporated into the domestic economic structure which conditions the appearance of parallel low-productivity activities whose social usefulness is dubious, among other features.

The intention behind the analysis so far made on some recent social trends was to show our approach to poverty as a many-sided phenomenon as opposed to the approaches pretending to restrict it to the number of people over or below a poverty (income) level—sometimes established under very personal criteria.

The poverty phenomenon must be considered as a manifestation of the segregation or exclusion suffered by whole nations or groups of people within a country whose potentialities are either not employed or are not allowed full development.

We consider poverty should above all be viewed from the qualitative angle. In this sense, poverty is related to the new capital accumulation-investment-reproduction model at a social level. It features a sui generis rationality consisting of taking advantage of those parts of the national economies that enable to maximize the profits at world level without having to integrate whole na-

38. PNUD, op. cit. , 85.

tions—understood as underdeveloped nations—into the great productive chain.

Due to the globalization process, such rationality does not only circumscribe to underdeveloped nations but also involves sectors of the developed world. Therefore the propagation of poverty is not restricted to the underdeveloped world but it is spreading over to some sectors of the industrialized nations considered "residual" or "surplus."

On that ground, one of the new angles of poverty is the fact that the present poor masses consist of both people that were already poor (endemic poverty, "old" poverty) and people that have recently become poor suffering severe socioeconomic conditions associated to the effects of putting into force structural adjustment policies ("fresh" poverty).

Likewise, the international economic context is contributing—now more than ever—to hinder the chances for people that were already poor to come out of poverty. Rather, in the present state of affairs, this kind of people is in a strong process leading to widespread reproduction of poverty conditions. Many researches have demonstrated poverty passes along from one generation to the next.

Both widespread poverty reproduction and its generational transmission result from the fact that individual standards of living within a given country are no longer solely influenced by economic, social and other personal means, and/or by those diverse conditions created by the nation states from their economic and financial means. The present globalization process—above all the globalization process of the world economy—determines the emergence of a great number of external variables influencing the living standards of individuals or groups of people.

The above is ascertained on studying the impact—and the relations—of the world-economy globalization process on the different aspects of socioeconomic conditions of the people as we will try to demonstrate hereinafter.

The synthetic nature of poverty—as a category allowing the social state at a given level to be summed up—manifests through the food problem, among other things.[39]

Food problems—especially those of the inhabitants in underdeveloped nations—may be approached from two points of view. On the one hand, the most general point of view is linked to the evolution of food production—output, productivity, domestic demand satisfaction rate by the national industry—and has something to do with land ownership and exploitation systems, degree of technical and scientific progress in the sector, diversification of agriculture and livestock production, and other factors. On the other hand, the most specific point of view is associated with the purchasing power of the individuals which is related to the possibility to acquire goods based on personal or family income levels, prices, among other variables.

Thus it is understandable that, regardless of the state of production—or better still, the state of food supply—in a given country, there is a very close relation between the individual standard of living (incomes) and his food situation.

Although it might not be generalized, one of the consequences of the structural adjustment policies the nations had to bear was the end of subsidies to manufacturing productions and the need to achieve surplus commercial balances through increased exports of their competitive productions, i.e., increased export concentration on a reduced number of basic products. As it has

39. Readers interested in the specific data that back up these conclusions may refer—among a wide bibliography on the subject—to FAO yearbooks: *El estado mundial de la agricultura y la alimentación* for 1980 and 1990.

been ascertained by numerous researches, it caused the restructuring of the production and the export system of agricultural produce in many underdeveloped countries —which in turn meant the appearance of a disequilibrium between the production-export structure and the domestic-consumption demand structure. Consequently, a gap developed, and it was somehow closed through importing food products at prices that might be higher than those of the domestic productions.

It seems that importing food products at prices higher than those of domestic productions has helped spread famine and malnutrition in underdeveloped nations, as some studies show.

Taking into account the objectives and logic limits of the present work, we cannot stop to examine the socioeconomic sequels and other consequences of the feeding deterioration of significant sectors in the underdeveloped world. However it must be noticed that—as stated above—reorienting the agricultural and livestock production structure increased the economic vulnerability of underdeveloped nations as their self-supply level is reduced and thus their food assurance is shaken.

Poverty and food problems in significant sectors of the underdeveloped world are closely related to public health. Although that relation is not a new one and has been broadly studied by academic circles and international organizations alike, it has gained renewed relevance due to quantitative and qualitative connotations.

On considering poverty as an aftereffect of some demographic trends, of the unemployment-underemployment-economy marginalization, and of food situation, it becomes the most direct cause of a serious sanitary situation characterized by propagation of already endemic diseases in the underdeveloped world, reappearance of diseases that either had been controlled or were on the way to be eradicated, and the outbreak and dangerous spread of new diseases.

So, when it is stated that poverty extension through the underdeveloped world is a threat to the developed regions of the world, it is necessary a many-sided approach to such a threat. It does not circumscribe to emigrants fleeing from progressively deteriorating socioeconomic conditions; it also involves the potential risk of irreversible natural disasters or uncontrolled epidemics that overflow the boundaries of the South and become worldwide problems.

Poverty is also manifested in the educational situation in underdeveloped nations. However many traditional analysis on the underdevelopment-education relations limited themselves to present—with a good deal of quantitativeness in the approach—the adverse effect of the educational situation on the possibilities for educational, technical and scientific, and cultural development for the masses in the underdeveloped world.

In current world development trends, human resources have a distinguished place. Such trends compel us to approach the underdevelopment-education relation through novel courses. It is no longer just a matter of a relation showing how some economic, political or other kind of actions—which lead to maintaining and deepening underdevelopment and poverty—become social-injustice situations due to the fact that the chances for the masses in the underdeveloped world to have access to adequate employment, education, food, living quarters, and health services are restricted. This would limit us to an ethical approach that however correct is not enough to evaluate the seriousness of some phenomena.

We consider that the increased disparity on national income distribution—mainly in underdeveloped countries—robs a great many people of a chance to develop their capacity and abilities, and to get better-paid jobs and better living standards. The cause of such a disparity is a huge concentration of wealth in a very reduced number of industrialized countries. But it is not just a question of blocking potential chances for a better life quality; the above-mentioned disparity not only promotes the reproduction of cheap and ill-qualified work force to comply with the globalization of the economic activity but also spoils the basis for the workers to eventually assimilate state-of-the-art technologies. It widens the technical and scientific gap which is becoming a valuable tool on the present competitive conditions and is perhaps the most relevant mechanism in present and future North-South relations.

The links between poverty and educational deficiencies, and the retrogression of state presence in seeing to a number of civil matters—due to lack of resources and adverse comments from some spheres—have helped propagate serious environment-deteriorating problems in many regions of the underdeveloped world.

Unlike developed nations, where environmental degradation is mostly related to industrial development and way-of-life patterns, in underdeveloped countries such a degradation is not even escorted by the palliative of increased number of goods and services to be enjoyed by the population for it features an attack upon the very bases of human survival: degradation of the soil, the water, and other natural resources.

Thus environmental degradation fosters interregional displacements within underdeveloped nations, emigration to neighboring nations, or to the North—with the ensuing transnationalization of the problem and the generation of tensions which started at the environmental sphere—have crossed over to the socioeconomic level, and might end up in the political sphere.[40]

40. Refer to ONU, *Informe*.

Instead of helping the détente of the international sociopolitical situation, the new international political context features the emergence and development of many social, ethical, and religious movements which seem to be the open expression of long-dormant problems, which could not be solved due to the seriousness of East-West contradictions and now surface randomly, and sometimes uncontrollably.

Together with the current international political trends, poverty propagation and deepening contribute to certain forms of sociopolitical movements occurring worldwide.

So one may conclude that, besides the traditional North-South contradictions, there are international, regional, and national factors that may be aiding a number of social movements more or less explosive or relevant to emerge beyond their native locations. To state it otherwise, contemporary world distinguishes by a great variety of sociopolitical movements in which many different agents participate. Such agents make it very difficult to follow the social and political alliances that have been forming around these movements. These sociopolitical movements are not only influenced by diverse international phenomena and processes but, in turn, influence their future evolution.

Perhaps the most unpredictable social trend is the disintegration appreciated in many societies resulting from the interweaving of many varied phenomena, processes, and trends—some of them already discussed.

For a long time now multiple reasons have been influencing the social disintegration process which developed societies are not exempt from—though it is better seen in underdeveloped societies because of its seriousness. Problems like violence and vandalism, narcotraffic and drug addiction, racism and xenophobia, proliferation of (pseudo)religious sects and diverse forms of fundamentalism are some of the prevailing manifestations which are helping social disintegration.[41]

Environmental Problems and Globalization Trends

After the warning call of considering environmental problems as a global affair, launched by the Club of Rome and the International Conference on Environment (Stockholm, 1972), humanity has gained gradual conscience of the need to preserve the environment as an invaluable prerequisite for its own survival.[42]

Although industrialized nations were taken to the defendant's seat when the environmental issue became a global concern because of their outstanding contribution to depletion of nonrenewable natural resources, water and air pollution, promotion of irrational consumption patterns and life styles, or their unfairly use of underdeveloped nations and collective areas of the planet as dumps for their toxic trash, nowadays they appear as the main promoters of altruistic environmental protection-related actions. Thus industrialized nations have introduced the subject in diverse international forums and have linked it to the most varied problems. They have insisted upon the adoption of ecology-friendly technologies, or have stood for the adoption of international environmental legislation.

This abrupt turn in the industrialized nations' public image on the subject of environmental protection is one

41. Some of these disintegration trends are analyzed in ONU, *Informe.*
42. D. Meadows et al. , op. cit.; M. Mesarovic and E. Pestel, op. cit.; and Naciones Unidas, *Informe de la Comisión Mundial sobre el Medio Ambiente y el Desarrollo (Nuestro futuro común).* (Nueva York: 1987), document A/42/427.

of the many manifestations of the change operated in international relations since the last decade as a consequence of the fall of East European regimes, the supposedly worldwide triumph of capitalism, the end of the East-West contradictions, and western pretensions to global expansion of its economic and sociopolitical organization patterns.

The environmental issue is a sui generis problem in the current international politico-ideological context. Although multiple and very serious trends in environmental deterioration—in the broadest sense of the term—can be seen, western political and academic circles are putting the environmental problem to their ends.

While the initial approaches to the environmental degradation featured a rather technocratic viewpoint, recent studies and researches have helped realize that beyond the strictly technical side of the question there are important interrelations concerning environmental-economic, sociopolitical and institutional problems. It reveals the ideological load of the environmental-degradation matter.

These interrelations of environment and economy and environment and society, environment and politics, and environment and institutions are being used by some western circles and international organizations to promote globalizing trends.

Environment-economy interrelations were highlighted as to criticize development patterns opposed to the preservation of nonrenewable natural resources which stimulated irrational consumption, or did not take into account the economic impact of such an action on the well-being of future generations. Today such interrelations are used by industrialized nations and some international organizations to create novel conditions to be fulfilled by the nations so their international action is considered adequate.

Thus, within GATT, discussions on the relations between environment and international trade have been held. There is also the precedent established by the United States related to the inclusion of a parallel environmentally-oriented treaty in the North American Free Trade Agreement.[43]

For that cause, instead of looking for a multilateral action to solve the ill effects that inadequate environmental policies might have in store for international trade relations, it seems to us that a group of nations—to serve their goals—has boosted specific actions as a sort of disguised protectionism against underdeveloped nations. These would probably be accused of *ecological dumping*—paraphrasing a term coined for other subject. Thus underdeveloped nations would turn out to be considered international criminals once declared violators of internationally-accepted environmental policies and regulations.

Two decades ago the main world powers were charged for being the principal polluters of the environment. At the time, problems like deforestation, desertification, and soil salinization were in a clear perspective. These problems were rightly considered logical consequences of backwardness and underdevelopment suffered by Third World countries which, in turn, derived from the traditional pillage and exploitation policies suffered at the hands of colonial and neocolonial powers.

But the "failure" of international cooperation and underdeveloped countries' governments to address environmental deterioration together with their incapability to reach acceptable levels of economic growth during the last decades has made a significant number of people to displace within the nation, or to emigrate to neighboring countries or to the North.

43. Refer to SELA/UNCTAD *Comercio y medio ambiente: el debate internacional* (Caracas: Editorial Nueva Sociedad, 1995).

Thus an environmental deterioration-poverty-emigration link has been established. In keeping with this, western powers have started to develop some tendentious thesis on the supposedly destabilizing effects such movements might have, and the need for international controlling measures to be adopted.

Once again—in the environment-society relations—the true causes explaining the underdevelopment-poverty-environmental deterioration-underdevelopment vicious circle are feigned to defend the conception that domestic socioeconomic problems in underdeveloped countries may originate worldwide unstableness.

Since world powers are taking important steps to make this notion accepted or validated, the political and institutional actions to enforce international would-be agreements are being rehearsed.

Therefore, due to the seriousness the environmental deterioration problem has come to, the environment-politics relation will not be considered as the need for the countries to undertake action-coordinating efforts to solve such problems as expression of putting in practice their political will.

Nowadays, when multilateralism is being replaced by forcible standpoints from the circles fostering globalizing trends, the environmental considerations are not truly oriented toward solving the problem but might turn out to be used as an economic or political tool against certain nations.

Thus we come to the environment-institutions relations. While two decades ago important agreements or institutional structures aiding environmental protection could not be reached or formed, the new international context has changed the standpoints of the main world powers on the matter.

In this sense, steps toward the creation of a superstructure intimately related to the rest of the pieces forming the international institutional network—which the main world powers are arranging to serve their globalizing aims—can be appreciated. There are also discussions on the need for developing international law by creating an environmental law.

Attention must be paid to the relevance given by western nations to the World Bank-linked Global Environmental Fund (GEF) as the international institution that will probably outline the strategies to be followed by the diverse countries and will channel funds to the detriment of the United Nations Environmental Program (UNEP)—which is the United Nations' agency for such purposes.

The environmental problem then becomes—together with human rights respect, minimum acceptable working conditions, and so on—one of the issues through which the main world powers are trying to show a new public image worldwide.

This apparent zeal from the "benevolent imperialism"—as it has been rightly called—has nothing to do with either altruism or real concern for the fulfillment of the goals agreed on for each issue. The true intentions are to create a new international juridical context according to the need for increased fostering of the globalizing trends, and so to elude occasional obstacles resulting from the nature of certain aspects of current international relations.[44] In keeping with this, it must be noticed the outcry the development of *ecology-friendly technologies* has provoked among industrialized nations and transnational corporations alike.

Environmental problems are directly or indirectly introduced in practically every international forum by developed nations. Hence, on referring to the development

44. For the development of this notion, refer to Roberto González Sousa and Pablo E. Chaviano Núñez, "Economía y medio ambiente, algunas consideraciones metodológicas", in *Investigaciones sobre medio ambiente* (FLACSO-Cuba/SODEPAZ, 1993).

process the specialized—and even the general—literature call it *ecologically sustainable development* to settle the fact that any process related to the satisfaction of human needs should avoid *ecological debts* to be paid by present or future generations.[45]

The seriousness of the main world powers' environmental projections is related to the fact that their pretensions are hidden behind the "noble issues," i.e., behind matters which have gained a deserved approval and hierarchy from international public opinion.

The pressures western powers have put on underdeveloped nations regarding environmental protection and collateral aspects are dangerous because they may be a pretext not only to justify the escalade of all sort of conditionings developed countries force on underdeveloped ones but also to eventually legitimate the creation of supranational mechanisms aimed at meddling in new aspects of underdeveloped nations' internal affairs.

During the 1980s and because of creditors' stubbornness, the governments of debtor underdeveloped nations received the debt-for-nature transaction as an acceptable partial solution. These operations however were denounced since the beginning because they interfered in underdeveloped countries' sovereignty over their natural resources as certain conditions were imposed upon them.

A higher step in this kind of meddling becomes evident from the pretensions of commissioning certain international entities the environmental protection and

45. On the subject—among a copious bibliography explaining this notion—, refer to the following documents: PNUD, *Informe de desarrollo humano,1994* (México: Fondo de Cultura Económica, 1994); idem, *Algunas preguntas y respuestas sobre el desarrollo humano sostenible* (s.l.: 1994); Jan Pronk Aud and Mabub ul Haq, *The Hague Report; Sustainable Development from Concept to Actions* (s.l.: 1992); and Silvio Baró Herrera, "El desarrollo sostenible: desafío para la humanidad." Typescript.

control of certain zones of the planet considered natural reserves for multiple species in danger of extinction.

Nonetheless we consider that behind the laudable initiative of preserving planet biodiversity western nations really hide their intention to avail themselves of a strategic natural resource rear guard whose future relevance cannot be predicted.

In recent times, the international agreements on reducing or eliminating gaseous emissions harming the ozone layer in a given lapse do not take into account the economic and financial differences of developed nations and underdeveloped nations to undertake modifications of equipment and productive processes.

This allows to realize one of the short-term goals lying behind the environmental proposals from the main world powers: being underdeveloped countries forced to modify equipment and productive processes as to satisfy international agreements, they are bound to import from the developed powers the ecologically-friendly technologies their transnational corporations have developed and capitalized on.

We consider those two examples on environmental issues are enough to show how sanctioning mechanisms are developing in the system of international relations.

World Political Trends— Their Potential Impact on the Situation of Underdeveloped Nations

The collapse of the socialist system brought about a peculiar "solution" for East-West contradictions, and great hopes to stop the irrational armament rush the world had witnessed over the post-World War II period, and so to put an end to the Cold War. It was expected that the end of the East-West contradictions and the end of the Cold War would enable a more just and more rational world order to be arranged.

However the above-mentioned way of "solving" East-West contradictions—through the dissolution of one of the contraries—caused an outburst of a triumphalistic euphoria in western power circles which aborted the development of realistic criteria about the best way to arrange the post-Cold War world.

Believing the collapse of the socialist camp was the irrefutable proof of the triumph of the capitalist system, defined the emergence and certain development of politico-ideological unipolarism. It tried to extrapolate the economic and sociopolitical model in force in western central countries to all nations in the planet without taking into account national criteria or specificities.

In truth, some manifestations of the attempts to enforce a single economic and sociopolitical pattern (which is a starting point for future unipolar trends) on all countries—or at least on underdeveloped nations—may be found in the adjustment policies promulgated by the IMF and the WB. They aspired to an identical policy—adopted by all underdeveloped nations—supposedly oriented toward solving the foreign-debt problem without caring for how a particular nation became indebted, how big the debt in question is, what level of relative development the country has, and other national conditions.[46]

Therefore unipolar standpoints reveal that many of the aspects that typified the Cold War are still in force. Instead of promoting a suitable climate for international negotiation, cooperation, and solidarity, conservative

46. These ideas are developed by Silvio Baró Herrera in "Las relaciones Norte-Sur a cincuenta años de la Conferencia de Bretton Woods," *Revista de Estudios Europeos* 31 (1994), edited by Centro de Estudios Europeos in Havana.

forces in power in many western countries have taken advantage of the present political juncture to boost force standpoints in international relations. Such standpoints do not differ from those during the Cold War.

The politico-ideological unipolarism that started to develop after the collapse of the socialist camp and the withdrawal of revolutionary or progressive forces practically all over the world have further rarified the international atmosphere. Whereas during the Cold War the fighting parties were rather well defined and the two superpowers applied themselves to recruiting those countries that kept themselves—or tried to anyway—out of the politico-ideological confrontation, nowadays whatever sign of economic or political independence on the part of any state is considered an "enemy" action to be eliminated in favor of a normal and steady development of the world system. The United States—pretending to become the triumphant and preponderant power of the emerging new world order—is the main actor of such an attitude.

On such conditions, politico-ideological unipolarism is not serious just because it is the expression of a very unfavorable turn in the international force correlation. It may be affirmed that in this context there is no counterbalancing power for the actions undertaken by a single (or many) power(s) to get to its (their) end(s). Perhaps the most important thing to remark is the fact that this situation enables—like no other time in the history of international relations—for the subjective conceptions and considerations of power circles in one or various countries to decisively influence the progress of international events. To say it otherwise: The present international junction features a significant increase in the relevance of the subjective factor (the will of political and other circles) not only on qualifying situations, phenomena, and processes but also on decision making.

From the economic angle, unipolarism has made itself be felt through the endeavors of the main world powers—especially the United States—to spread the neoliberal pattern all over the world. They have been supported by international financing organizations—the IMF and the WB—due to the extremely important role these have played on designing, enforcing, and controlling the so-called structural adjustment policies.

This stage of unipolarism does not circumscribe to try to homogenize the (macro)economic policies employed in almost all (underdeveloped) countries; it is also characterized by rasing the relevance of diverse criteria and indexes used to evaluate economic results. Thus considerations such as cost-benefit, profitability, efficiency, market play, prices, and other market economy categories have acquired an a priori credibility because they escort the economic policies imposed by the central powers and their international organizations.

From the political angle, one of the most important manifestations of unipolarism is the industrialized nations' pretensions to extrapolate worldwide their sociopolitical organization model and their institutional system. The promotion of this homogenization attempt—which will be studied further on in more detail—started two decades ago and has gone through diverse stages.

The actions undertaken by current world power centers do not only seek to uniform the economic, social, and political aspects. As a logical derivation from this fact, such centers also seek certain homogenization of cultural criteria and conceptions, and value systems for they are necessary aspects to complete the globalization process in all orders.

To achieve cultural homogenization the world powers have not only been backed up by a favorable international context but also by state-of-the-art developments in communications, transportation, and other fields.[47]

Cultural homogenization becomes a valuable goal in the current globalization process. To reach such aim —sometimes narrowly considered as the expansion of consumption markets—it is promoted for peoples in most different countries to adopt western value systems. It would make such peoples play the role of receivers of goods and services from central economies. Thus the attempts to homogenize the economic policies applied in diverse countries, sociopolitical patterns, institutional structures, and worldwide extension of cultural conceptions and western value systems are some of the steps undertaken by the central powers to create a more-globalization-favorable international and national milieu.

The globalization goal—whatever the approach to the subject—is opposed to the real existence of a variety of nation states and their corresponding frontiers. The approach to the globalization phenomenon as promoted by the central powers considers national states and national frontiers its most important obstacle. Against them theoretical and conceptual actions are directed to demonstrate their obsolescence, the unfeasibility of some states, and the convenience to form bigger political and economic units.

On reviewing the statements on structural adjustment policies defended by neoliberal theorists, the criticism against the state attracts attention. The state is charged with exceeding its functions on intervening broadly, inefficiently, and wrongly upon economy; establishing bureaucratic structures; carrying out actions which—instead of fostering economic growth—helped

47. Refer to C. Ominami, ed., *La tercera revolución industrial* (Buenos Aires: Grupo Editorial Latinoamericano, 1986).

the stagnation of productive sectors and putting into force paternalistic social policies.

It has been rumored about the need for the state to withdraw and to be replaced by private entrepreneurs. However those very same voices do not say the State had to assume those duties in order (to try) to dynamize depressed national economies, or those on which private entrepreneurs did not wish to risk their capital.

The attack is particularly vicious against the states of underdeveloped nations. It is misleading on the real and objective causes for state deficiencies—lack of qualified cadres, incipient nature of the state apparatus, corruption, and so on.

Besides the criticism voiced by ruling circles in western countries on the national states of underdeveloped nations, hides the fact that the volume of the bureaucratic structure in underdeveloped nations and other current problems are consequences of the colonial policy western countries enforced.

Together with the criticism of the structural-adjustment neoliberal-policies, reconsiderations on the first attacks upon the states and the urgent need for their downsizing have emerged. They are imperative conditions of the set of measures promoted by Breton Woods's institutions. Hence, it is commented that the state as such must be re-created, and its functions reanalyzed on the new national and international conditions; i.e., the state role is being revitalized, which introduces a contradictory element into globalization goals.[48]

We consider that the western countries' globalizing conceptions seem to move in three parallel levels. Firstly, apologies of the processes leading to the formation of great economic-commercial blocks and of the

48. Bernardo Kliksberg, comp., *El rediseño del Estado: Una perspectiva internacional* (México: Fondo de Cultura Económica, 1994).

European-Union-like integrating schemes are made. These are shown as processes matching current world trends. In keeping with this, such globalizing conceptions boost—and grant an exaggerated credibility to —supranational mechanisms which are considered the panacea for eventual decision making on global problems.

Secondly, globalizing conceptions demand nation states weakening as to help attain the final goal. Such a weakening has been attempted through not only the reduction of the scope of state functions—and consequently its size—but also by displacing it from the principal economic activities, debating on the unfeasibility of small states, and developing theses to demonstrate that the permanence of nation states and borderlines are anachronisms attempting against the current development trends of international political and economic relations.

Thirdly, globalizing trends are also based on weakening the state via decentralizing its functions, i.e., by conceding greater decision-making power to subnational levels, and strengthening the so-called civil society. Thus the cohesive role of the national interests and the representative role of such domestic interests before other States that should be performed by national States, are disappearing. The cohesive role would be performed by nongovernmental and social organizations and others while the representative role would be assumed by supranational levels.[49]

Resulting from the alleged obsolescence and anachronism of nation states—nation state weakening as we view it—, central powers will be able to carry out their globalizing and homogenizing strategies more easily.

The western approach to globalization—from the criterion that some nation states are unfeasible as a consequence of their size, relative economic and political

49. For the matter we recommend PNUD, *Informes de desarrollo humano, 1993 and 1994.*

110

importance, stability, governability, and other factors —implies that the decision making on the most relevant world problems is concentrated on a reduced number of countries, i.e., the great powers. These will design, enforce and control the strategies and policies to be adopted seemingly to address such problems.

Although the European Union cannot as yet be presented as a successful performance example of supranational mechanisms, its experiences have conveniently aided the ends of western powers' political circles which need to introduce institutional levels more adapted to the current globalization process. These institutions would replace the "anachronistic" or "unfeasible" nation states.

Thus the relevance assigned to supranational mechanisms for decision making is an interesting trend in the current international political relations. Two paths can be appreciated in this particular international political trend. The first one—from a chronological point of view —is related to the formation of supranational organizations from integrating schemes in developed countries (the above-mentioned case of the European Union may be an example), or the formation of economic-commercial blocks, like NAFTA which involves developed and underdeveloped countries. The second one lies in actions toward the formation of supranational levels derived from existing international organizations; it may also involve creating new organizations or restructuring existing ones.

Although in recent documents or oral statements the discarding of previous versions is emphasized, we consider that the second one toys with the idea of forming a world governance. Hence ideas on how the prospective supranational levels could perform legislative, executive, and judicial—even repressive—functions to safeguard the world order stability have been stated.[50]

50. Refer to PNUD, *Informe 1992*.

Supranationality as fostered by the western approach to the globalization process is based on two features: on the one hand, the concentration—as never before in history—of the economic, commercial, financial, technical and scientific, and military power in a reduced number of central powers; on the other hand, the emergence and development of a phenomenon opposed to globalization: *exclusion*.[51]

More or less cunningly the institutional mechanism to be put into force to spur supranationality will exclude or segregate a significant number of nations from the decision-making process on the main global problems, regardless which supranationality trend is assumed.

What has been so far stated might lead to believe supranational mechanisms are wholly negative. It might be due to the way western political circles have approached the globalization phenomenon and have developed diverse conceptions and arguments toward its practical implementation.

As stated above, globalization is an objective trend along world development. It is imposing on politicians, academic circles, and general public the need for the best methods and ways to regulate international relations and decision making in a globalized-world context. But it must be done from a version grounded on cooperation and solidarity among nations involved in order to answer adequately the multiple problems humanity is facing, or those it might encounter in the future. However—at least for the time being—the present international context favors the formation of the new world order the main world powers—especially the United States—desire.

Consequently, together with the actions oriented to weakening nation states and promoting supranational

51. Refer to Silvio Baró Herrera, "Globalización y exclusión." Typescript.

mechanisms to regulate international relations, there is another trend. It consists of the insistence of the main world powers on conferring credibility to the statement that a convenient process of globalization—which would be advantageous for all nations involved—demands from each country to surrender part of its national sovereignty so the supranational levels may perform their duties better.

The thesis on *limited sovereignty* results in one of the most controversial questions in modern political actions and statements for its acceptance would undermine the very basis of states. Besides, the idea of surrendering part of national sovereignty is received with much suspiciousness and reticence by underdeveloped countries. These countries regard the idea of surrendering part of national sovereignty as a reproduction of the subordination and dependency on developed nations suffered during colonial dominance and not completely overcome even after political independence.

As it will be explained hereinafter, the ideas of limited sovereignty and pan-national *corresponsibility* regarding world problems have made underdeveloped countries realize the new international conditions have not brought about a favorable change for them; on the contrary, an increase in North-South disparities is appreciated. These could on the one hand cause North-South contradictions to increase, and on the other hand new international commitments for underdeveloped countries—obligations which do not take into consideration underdeveloped countries' relative development levels and other peculiarities.[52]

The notion of limited sovereignty involves a remarkable retrogression relative to well-known standards and

52. On how underdeveloped nations have been gradually losing the differential treatment they had formerly enjoyed and have contracted new international obligations, refer to Baró Herrera, "El desarrollo sostenible." Tapescript.

principles regulating international relations. While the spirit prevailing over the first few decades after World War II was prone to recognize the relative development disparities between developed and underdeveloped countries and requested a differential treatment for the latter, the present trend deserts the most elemental criteria for international solidarity. So it is considered that the implications derived from surrendering part of the sovereignty would be similar for each group of countries.

The new international context we have been dealing with has another trend: the emergence and development of *new forms of meddling*.

The central powers have taken advantage of the many-sided nature of the cardinal world problems humanity faces—i.e., economic, social, environmental, and political problems—to undertake actions to regulate international relations.

While the emergence and introduction of new forms of meddling into international relations have not meant replacing its more traditional mechanism, associated to previous stages of the world capitalist system evolution, it is convenient to remark the unusual progress such new forms have attained, their subtle nature, and the fact that they are likely to gain a privileged place in the actions performed by the great powers and international organizations.

We consider that the old forms of meddling basically practiced against underdeveloped nations were a resource of the main industrialized nations on Cold War conditions. They were meant to destabilize governments considered hostile to the interests of the industrialized nations, or to make them fall, or were just a way to hinder the actions of such governments. Thus, industrialized nations were after political changes in nations which were favorable to western interests as to turn over the international force correlation.

Nowadays, before the collapse of the East European bloc and the former USSR, the main world powers consider that significant and very strong centripetal forces tending to make the underdeveloped countries move around the three great centers of world power have started to move. It has enabled the world powers to unleash new meddling forms trying to adequate underdeveloped nations to the ends of the globalization process rather than causing political changes.

The new meddling shapes up as conditionings imposed upon underdeveloped countries by industrialized nations or international organizations.

The first steps taken by western powers to introduce diverse conditionings as a new form of meddling were noticed in the economic field. Hence the industrialized-nations' Generalized Systems of Preferences —since their initial versions—contemplated that underdeveloped nations would only be eligible should they fulfilled a number of economic—and also political—conditions. Thus the idea of a system of standards and other regulations easing the access of underdeveloped nations to industrialized nations' markets was spoiled since its origins because the system was not generally intended after all. On the one hand, all underdeveloped countries were not eligible; on the other hand, not all the goods exported by underdeveloped nations gained free access to developed countries' markets.

After the foreign-debt crisis erupted at the beginning of the last decade and due to the fact underdeveloped countries needed a more or less permanent access to capital markets as to fill their financial obligations, these countries faced an escalade of conditionings. First of all, creditors stipulated that to renegotiate the debt and to undertake other actions aiming at its solution underdeveloped nations had to get approval of the IMF first, and later of the IMF and the WB. IMF coming into the picture brought about enforcing the adjustment policies and other conditionings stipulated by the IMF and the WB for debtor countries.

A feature of the new conditionings western powers have imposed upon underdeveloped nations is that in many occasions concessions whose nature differs from the advantage these nations requested are demanded —to say nothing about the imbalance between what is received and what is delivered. Therefore, revisions of the Generalized Systems of Preferences not only toughened and made the eligibility conditions more restrictive but also introduced the possibility of demanding social or political conditions—human rights respect, free trade-unionism for workers, democracy demands, multipartism, etc.

Launching the pro-human rights respect campaign created the basis for the emergence of a new kind of conditionings imposed by the developed countries upon underdeveloped ones. Thus, in the current bilateral and multilateral relations, it can be commonly found that human rights respect is a prerequisite for a given underdeveloped nation to gain access to credits, loans, some sort of commercial advantage, or just to be allowed to sign a treaty or agreement.

In keeping with this, it is enough to note the evolution of the European Union's agreements with nonsignatory countries. Currently its treaties with other—generally underdeveloped—countries have as an ever-present feature, some prerequisite related to human rights respect and democracy promotion.

The fact that world public opinion recently became aware of environmental degradation enables to use this issue as an additional conditioning to force upon under-developed nations. Therefore, in bilateral and multilateral treaties and agreements, it may be noticed that when (underdeveloped) nations are granted a certain economic or financial benefit, they should undertake environment-preservation actions.

During the final sessions of GATT's Uruguayan Round of Multilateral Commercial Negotiations, the United States launched a controversial idea which has been called the *social clause*. The intention of this notion—which the remaining industrialized nations have started to follow up—is to condition interstate commercial relations—understood as developed nations-underdeveloped nations commercial relations—to underdeveloped countries compliance with the international labor legislation in force. Behind it, many experts infer a new variant of neoprotectionism on the part of developed countries—which consider themselves threatened by the competitive levels reached by some underdeveloped countries in the production of certain goods that the central powers are interested in.[53]

Since the mid-1970s academic circles started up a reevaluation process of conventional theories on development. As a result of that, the approaches which stressed the importance of techno-economic factors were dropped in favor of those emphasizing the socioeconomic factors.[54]

Lately, a significant progress in the conceptualization process of this new approach to development has been appreciated. The most important element of the new

53. Refer to Silvio Baró Herrera, "La cláusula social," *Trabajadores* (Havana)(May 1994).
54. From the remarkable exercise carried out by academic circles in many latitudes we shall just highlight the thesis on "the other development." Refer to *Development Dialogue* 1-2 (1975).

thesis is considering the human being not only as the object of development but also the subject of it.

It seems that this kind of approach to the development issue was related to the main direction of the most rigorous criticisms against neoliberal policies which have been characterized by limiting themselves almost exclusively to search for the equilibrium among the main macroeconomic aggregates, the free play of market forces, and the reduction of the economic role of the state, among other goals. Thus, these policies completely bypass social consequences.

However, the economic reality of each country, the aforementioned policies were applied in showing that the rigor of the measures involved in the structural adjustment policies caused dreadful social consequences which have been referred to hereinbefore.

From which has been so far stated it follows that, within the latest political trends, those relative to the role and place of the individual stand out. On this matter, diametric positions may be observed. On the one hand, the position of western political circles which defend the thesis of the respect for human rights and fundamental liberties—thesis restricted to civil and political rights—, and hyperbolically support the idea of the human being as an individual. On the other hand, the position of the progressive circles which state that economic, social, and cultural rights should stand together—and be assured along—with civil and political rights. Both sets of rights form an indivisible and interdependent unit which is an approach to the idea of the human being as a social being.

At first glance it might just seem a divergence on the way the individual issue is approached, but in truth behind that seemingly simple question lie others being more profound and relevant—the emphasis on the human being as an individual plays an important role not only for promoting the neoliberal economic model and extrapolating worldwide the western sociopolitical system but also for granting credibility to freedom of action as a principle which supposedly works for both economy and society; the socioeconomic fate of each individual depends on his own efforts as if other forces or agents were not involved; the full realization of the human being is reached on enjoying certain rights and liberties which in many cases are abstract and ambiguous when they are dealt with outside concrete historical contexts.[55]

On the contrary, when the emphasis is laid on the human being as a social being the approach is more many-sided because it is not solely viewed as an isolated, particular entity but in its interrelations with the rest. This two-level analysis of the human being and the respect for its rights makes it possible to understand that respecting some human rights goes along with respecting others. So to enable some groups of individuals to achieve the respect of their whole share of rights, it is necessary to create the conditions for other groups of individuals to become aware of the need to respect the rights of third parties. It means that the rights that should be respected at world level are not just the individuals' rights but also those of groups of individuals, and nations. This aspect is avoided by those who emphasize respecting the human rights of the individuals—which is not only a very narrow approach to the matter but also (and above all) a contradictory one in a world where there are factions willing the states to disappear and the creation of supranational levels to regulate international relations.

The western campaign in favor of human rights respect launched during the second half of the 1970s acquired new connotations with the offensive in favor of

---

55. Refer to Silvio Baró, "Derechos humanos, desarrollo y Nuevo Orden Mundial," *Informes Especiales* (December 1994), edited by Centro de Estudios Europeos in Havana.

democracy and multipartism. Through the troika, *human rights respect-democratization-multipartism*, western powers have gained a significant weapon to put pressure firstly on the nations that belonged to the former Eastern bloc, and presently on underdeveloped countries.

It is not an exaggeration to state that the above-mentioned campaign has become an outstanding milestone for the main world powers to influence the evolution of international political relations. While the pro-human rights respect campaign was meant to directly influence the course of national events—and indirectly influence world events—, the new approach has meant a strategy modification and is now oriented to search for a direct many-sided influence upon both national and international events.

Hence the dangerous consequences derived from this approach of the western powers to influence the design and evolvement of international political relations because this approach appears after military governments gave way to democratic regimes in many underdeveloped nations—like those in Latin America—, and when the collapse of the socialist countries is just shown as a consequence of lack of democracy.

Thus the call for human rights respect, democracy, and multipartism has not just gained an enormous credibility worldwide but it has been possible for western powers to turn their own goals into world goals by introducing them in all international forums—in those belonging to the United Nations system and intergovernmental organizations alike.

Therefore, international political relations are conditioned by a kind of dogma according to which human rights respect is only feasible on the basis of democratically established societies, i.e., western-styled societies. And such a democracy is only possible when there are many political parties, which supposes options and diversity.

As it can be easily understood, this request for human rights respect, democratization, and multipartism (politico-ideological diversity) is placed over underdeveloped nations by the central powers, and it is part of the pressure actions undertaken by the latter to weaken nation states, or to shape them up after globalization interests.

A closer look shows that a real and general respect for human rights is not the goal—neither overall democratization or a complete flourishing of politico- ideological exchange worldwide—because it would not aid the globalization ends of western nations.

One thing is the (rhetorical) campaign promoted by politico-ideological circles, a different thing altogether is the international reality. Over the last few years international reality has featured the violation of (human) rights in whole nations, a substantial retrogression of democratic actions—mainly those of international organizations—, and a search for the uniformity of political and ideological conceptions, value systems, and consumption patterns, whatever the cost may be.

Such a contradiction between the national and international field, between rhetoric and reality, is a substantial contradiction in the present international political order which shows a fissure whose consequences are unforeseeable.

In keeping with a previous analysis, it must be indicated that not only the evaluation made by industrialized nations on human rights respect is taken into account to grant certain economic advantage or benefit but also the steps taken by the governments to democratize—western-style—their societies and "conveniently" reform their political systems.

It means that industrialized nations continue to accumulate new elements that enable them to meddle in the internal political affairs of other (underdeveloped) nations. Such has been the degree of influence reached by the centers of world power over the political systems of other nations that some circles devoted themselves to create indexes to evaluate the political situation in the countries, and to make a sort of world ranking regarding the respect for human rights and other essential liberties.

So we reach another trend appreciated in the current international political relations: The attempt by the main world powers to set rigorous patterns—either directly or through international organizations—to be followed by the diverse countries related to political, economic, social, and other aspects.

This trend manifests itself through the proliferation of studies on establishing or introducing indexes—or sets of indexes—which allow to monitor previously agreed-upon or imposed policies to reach certain ends.

It seems that the sad success obtained by creditor powers and the institutions of Bretton Woods over the debtor (underdeveloped) nations settled a deplorable precedent regarding the possibility to impose from the outside patterns and indexes to be followed by underdeveloped nations under certain conditions.

Besides the macroeconomic rates underdeveloped countries should comply with to get a positive evaluation from the IMF and the WB, and to be able to negotiate with creditor states and banks, the political and academic circles of western powers and some international organizations have worked on the creation of a system of indexes to keep an eye on the economic, political, and social situation in underdeveloped nations. Within this set of efforts the so-called Index of Human Development (IHD) created by UNIDO stands out due to the diffusion it has gained.[56]

56. Refer to PNUD, *Informe de desarrollo humano, 1990* (Bogotá: Tercer Mundo Editores, 1990).

However, the idea of indexes to monitor the internal situation in underdeveloped countries is a manifestation of a trend that has been developing since the last years of the 1980s and the beginning of the 1990s. This new trend consists of the attempt to structure a many-sided conception to support an *integral meddling* in the internal affairs of the countries.

For some time now such a conception has been linked to the promotion of the notion of *good governance—good management*—through which the countries should comply with certain foreign requests so their governments could be considered good ones and so be able to get foreign aid, be eligible for bank loans, become potential destinations for foreign investments, and many other "benefits" of that kind.

The idea of good governance goes hand in hand with the above-mentioned indexes that could serve to measure diverse country performances. However, should we consider the indexes so far presented, we will find no special regard for the degree of relative development or any other national peculiarity. It makes us realize such a notion will act directly on the homogenizing ideas discussed at the beginning of this chapter.

Globalization and Institutionalization

Along with the changes derived from the diverse world trends studied in the preceding chapters, some supposedly necessary institutional transformations are being promoted.

The so-called old international order—on its way to being replaced—emerged at a historical moment characterized by (a) the existence of a world consisting of dozens of nations—some of them with a long-standing independent life, come others with a short-lived independence—; (*b*) a tendency to consolidation of the state, independence, sovereignty, and self-determination; (*c*) the shaping up of an intergovernmental system of international organizations headed by the United Nations and its specialized agencies, and complemented by a number of other international and regional institutions; and (*d*) a certain degree of internationalization of the economic life resulting from the magnitude gained by international economic relations, the expansion of transnational companies, and the progress achieved by the schemes for economic integration and cooperation, among other features.

Other important characteristic of the world order in the Cold-War-era was the ideologization of international political and economic relations resulting from the division of the world in two sociopolitical systems. Such an ideologization sometimes resulted in the existence of more than one organization or institution to regulate international relations of a given kind. While there was a single United Nations system and a single institution or agency specialized in a particular field, two situations could be found: (*a*) the presence of—at that time—the European Economic Community (EEC) and the Council for Mutual Economic Assistance (CMEA) as integration and/or economic cooperation schemes in Europe, and the North Atlantic Treaty Organization (NATO) and the Warsaw Treaty Organization (WTO) as strategic and military mechanisms of the bipolar confrontation in Europe; and (*b*) the existence of international organizations without a socialist counterpart—as was the case of the IMF, the WB, and the GATT. Although a few socialist countries belonged to such organizations, the rest was not involved in that sphere of international negotiations.

The international post-World War II institutional system became still more complex due to other two reasons. The member countries from some regions of the planet considered that the best way to discuss and to solve the problems of a particular zone was not in the context of far-reaching multilateral organizations. So, in the international arena, agencies and organizations that dealt with the problems pertaining to each region began to proliferate. For that cause, there are organizations for political, economic, financial, and other problems. As simple examples of the vast spectrum of entities that may be found in the different regions of the world, there are the Organization of American States (OAS), the Organization for Cooperation and Economic Development, and the Bank for African Development (BAFD). The United Nations itself contributed to such a proliferation through the creation of some regional economic commissions.

The second reason for the complexity of the international post-war institutional system lies in the fact that a lot of underdeveloped nations kept away from both the confrontation between the great superpowers and their attempt to develop particular ways to coordinate their criteria on politics and economy in international forums. Such an attitude of underdeveloped countries would lead firstly to the foundation of the Movement of Non-Aligned Countries, and later on to the development of certain structures within international organizations or United Nations agencies, like the Group of 77.[57]

57. For an analysis of the place of the Movement of Non-Aligned Countries and the Group of 77 within the international institutional system, refer to G. Bondarerski and V. Sofinski, *La no alineación: sus amigos y adversarios en la política mundial* (Moscow: Ciencias Sociales Contemporáneas 1979); Slavko Stanic, *La no alineación y el nuevo orden económico internacional* (Belgrade: *Cuestiones actuales del socialismo*, 1979); K. Ramamurthy and Govind Narain Srivastava, *NAM Today* (Institute for Non-Aligned Studies, 1985); *Non-Alignment in the Eighties* (Belgrade: Institute of International Politics and Economics, 1982); and Karl P. Sauvant, *El Grupo de los 77: evolución, estructura, organización* (Havana: Ministerio de Comercio Exterior, n.d.).

As it may be understood, this heterogeneity within the international institutional system would neither enable to analyze the problems and to make decisions on them quickly, nor be properly efficient.

On modifying old statements leading to restructuring the United Nations system—due to the relevance of this organization and its specialized agencies—the main world powers have capitalized on this idea to make it serve their globalization ends.

In our opinion, the position of the principal underdeveloped countries with respect to the restructuring process of the United Nations may be grouped in two stages. The first one is typified by the over-critical attitudes of the United States during the 1970s, which were not always followed by the rest of the western countries. As a consequence of this and thanks to the votes of underdeveloped countries, some resolutions disagreeing with U.S. interests were passed. It made the principal world power complain of "politicization of the debates" and "majority's dictatorship."

These were the years of the Declaration and Action Program for a new international economic order, the Charter on Economic Duties and Rights of the States, and a number of special periods of the United Nations General Assembly in which diverse issues of great interest to underdeveloped nations were amply discussed —among the relevant issues were raw materials, development, and international cooperation.[58]

During this stage the attitude of the United States was that of blackmailing the United Nations by threatening to quit UN agencies or stop paying the quota, should U.S. criteria were not accepted. During this stage the at-

58. For an analysis of the United Nations system during this period and the relative importance of these documents, refer to Silvio Baró, *El nuevo orden económico internacional: antecedentes, problemas actuales y perspectivas* (Havana: Editorial de Ciencias Sociales, 1980).

tempts to discredit UN functions were also obvious by removing from the United Nations system the most important international issues at the time and discussing them in reduced circles whose composition was more favorable to U.S. interests.

Thus it must be recalled that, while it was difficult to get U.S. agreement to hold the so-called Global Economic Negotiations within the United Nations, the United States co-sponsored other endeavors for international negotiations—the North-South Dialogue (1975-1977), and the Cancun Conference (1981). During that same period U.S. strategy boycotted those United Nations agencies or organizations whose work was considered bias—a leaning toward the interests of some groups of countries—, or interfering in U.S. efforts to strengthen certain international organizations. Take for example U.S. attacks upon UNCTAD, its quitting UNESCO, and its steps to increase GATT's world relevance since the seventies.

The second stage of the developed countries position relative to the United Nations started sometime in the 1980s when—due to the obvious internal crisis of socialist nations and their concentration on domestic problems—the developed countries took the initiative and have set the course and controlled the speed of the changes they want in the United Nations system.

Contrary to the strategy followed during the 1970s, the strategy fostered since the 1980s manifests itself in diverse levels while its nature is subtler and more sophisticated than the preceding one.

One of the levels of the strategy could be considered a continuity or a new step of the first-stage strategy. It consists of trying to "rationalize" both the number of specialized agencies and organizations belonging to the United Nations system and the amount of functions they perform by transferring functions from some organizations or agencies to others.

The most clear example of this angle of the second-stage strategy is U.S. attempt to originally reduce —and if possible to eliminate—UNCTAD since the beginning of the 1980s and then to add to the GATT some functions from UNCTAD, the World Industrial Property Organization, and other specialized agencies.

A close examination of the so-called Uruguay Round of Multilateral Commercial Negotiations within the GATT (1986-1994)—together with the traditional negotiating process to liberalize international trade—shows that through it the main world powers achieved the refurbishment of GATT. Now it is more globally related to both membership and scope of issues. It must be noticed that the Uruguay Round had much wider connotations as fresh issues were discussed.

In this sense, the World Trade Organization (WTO) —GATT's heir—has the outstanding merit of being the first international organization where the main world powers could express their rationalizing ideas. It must be realized however that the newly-born entity not only served the globalization ends pursued by the world powers—those ends for which a more representative, a more far-reaching, and above all a more world-power-controlled trade organization was required—but also favored the integrality, the systematization, and the many-sided approach of commercial problems. The WTO was to deal with not only all essential matters related to assets and services but also those regarding investments and copyright.

An example of the creation of a new organization could be put. Some circles state that the United Nations system as it stands today is somehow "underdeveloped" as far as socioeconomic development is concerned.

There are also statements on the need for increasing the relevance of the social issues.

The idea of restructuring the system is grounded on the criterion that the attention to world socioeconomic problems is dispersed over a vast spectrum of specialized agencies whose funds belong to the United Nations: Such an arrangement rests efficiency and hinders quick decision making. Such alleged deficiencies would be solved by creating the Security Council for Development—also called Economic Security Council—which would be ruled by a reduced number of countries—just like the United Nations Security Council—in charge of drawing up the strategies to be followed by the rest.[59]

The second level of the standpoints of the developed countries related to the process of United Nations restructuring is the most complex and consists of short-term and medium-term actions. This level suggests a revitalization of the role played by the United Nations and other international organizations to form a similar entity or a world governance.[60]

The above statement must be joined to the fact that the Security Council has—now more than ever before—become a tool of the five permanent members. Diverse resolutions on embargoes, use of military force or supposedly humanitarian aid passed by the Security Council are some examples of the "novel actions" undertaken by this United Nations organ which has acquired such unheard-of relevance that it has even nullified the role of the General Assembly in a gross violation of the Charter of the United Nations.

Should the Security Council for Development (or Economic Security Council) be created and should the actions of the present Security Council continue, the main

59. For ideas on the creation of a Security Council for Development, refer to PNUD, *Informe 1992*.
60. For ideas on a world governance, see note 59.

world powers would achieve the high degree of institutionalization of supranational mechanisms required by the globalization ends.

In this second stage, the steps toward restructuring the United Nations and other international levels—which could form a sort of world governance—also lead to strengthening the legal functions of the United Nations, and creating new punitive functions as to maintain the stability and governability demanded by the new world order desired by the centers of world power.

In the documents *A Peace Program* and *Supplement to a Peace Program* by Boutros Boutros-Ghali, secretary-general of the United Nations, the intentions to furnish the system with mandate and means to attain the above-mentioned goals are doubtlessly expressed.

The United States
—How to Attain Leadership and Hegemony in the New World Order?

Once the Cold War ended, the pillars which the U.S. national security doctrine was erected upon crumbled for it was based on the principle of being in conflict with the U.S.S.R and international communism after World War II. Not only was this security doctrine operative for the U.S. performance on the world scenario but also acted as a cohesive element for the developed capitalist world led by the United States.

So, bipolarity disappearance has brought to the forefront of world issues the interimperialist economic and North-South contradictions, both at regional and global scale. Under such circumstances, the United States needs a new doctrinal basis from which to wield its leadership over the capitalist world and its hegemony over South countries.

Consequently, to define *the new conception of U.S. security* today it is necessary to conjugate adequately: (a) the economic preeminence in a highly competitive context based on U.S. interests diverging from those of U.S. allies in Europe and Japan plus the challenges derived from political destabilization in east Europe—recession, rebirth of interethnic hatred, religious fundamentalism, xenophobia—; and (b) the humanity-related problems which must be solved to assure the stability of the sys-

tem of international relations—narcotraffic, nuclear proliferation, environmental deterioration, population and
migration growth, extreme wealth disparities. Summing
up, in spite of the fact that the United States is a North
country, the new globalization trends mean a process of
redefining both its international position and the mechanisms, tools and scenarios to continue exercising its
past preeminent status within world capitalism.

The new U.S. security doctrine—as it is a global dominance project—demands a differential treatment for
each region of the planet. This is because the U.S. specific interest in each region, the degree of application,
and the potential success—depending on the goals and
the challenges—must be taken into account. Therefore,
three levels of application of the global project to be
structured can be identified.

A UNITED EUROPE

Among the diverse issues whose strategic and military connotation is highly relevant, the United States
must pay prioritized attention to the restructuring of
NATO, its relations with Russia, the nuclear threat, and
the disadvantage suffered by the U.K.-U.S. alliance due
to the emergence of France and Germany as two powers
likely to exert leadership in Europe. However, the main
challenge to U.S. leadership today is its being able to
root such leadership on solid economic grounds.

ASIA-PACIFIC

Japanese increased self-sufficiency—even in military
terms—, the accelerated growth of the Chinese economy, the consolidation of the Asian Tigers, and the process of creating a commercial block in the Pacific area
—among others—mean a potential loss of the influence
the United States has enjoyed since the 19th century.

Future events may follow two courses. Either the United States, Japan and China harmoniously participate in conforming their economic interests, or the United States is excluded from an area which might be controlled by a China-Japan agreement. The United States' will to avoid losing the position it holds in the region has obvious manifestations in its policy toward Vietnam and China.

The world area called Third World under bipolarity conditions must be reconceptualized as a consequence of the development of new—mainly economic—trends. Thus, while it must be taken into account that typical manifestations of underdevelopment belong to Latin America and Africa, its features in Europe and the Asia-Pacific area cannot be disregarded. This problem demands reconsidering the indexes to consider a certain country or region as part of the South—as opposed to the North—in the development-underdevelopment dichotomy, regardless of the economic and social growth models applied.

SOUTH

Because of the historical development level of Latin America, this region has traditionally occupied a relevant place within the so-called Third World.

Its location in the U.S. immediate sphere of influence determines a position in the hegemony project which has relevant aspects for U.S. national security with a high degree of geopolitics, geostrategy, and ideology involved.

Controlling the area is imperative for the United States to exercise its leadership in the North and its hegemony over the South. Therefore its organic integration with Latin America depends—as befitting the current times—on its economic needs. Consequently, the domination scheme must be applied in its highest degree, i.e., harmonizing the model of neoliberal economy and restricted democracy as the only way to adequate Latin-American economy to the imperatives of an economic bloc while maintaining the necessary political stability.

Other degree of employing the U.S. domination scheme refers to Africa. The absence of strategic interests in the African region enables more laxness on using the mechanisms contemplated in the above-mentioned scheme.

The persistent relations of the African countries with their former European metropolises make it possible for issues like Maghreb and—in a good measure—those related to the sub-Saharan area to be controlled via "cooperation" between the United States and Europe by applying multilateral control formulas—allocation of funds, credits, loans—through international institutions like the International Monetary Fund, the World Bank, and those belonging to the United Nations system like UNIDO, and others.

Identifying the application levels of the U.S. global project based on a new North design makes it necessary to study the possible course of the system of international relations.

The current state of unipolarism resulting from the disappearance of the USSR represents a transition process of the system of international relations toward new arrangement forms. Such a statement takes into account U.S. limitations and potentialities to turn this transition period into a permanent historical situation. Consequently, in the U.S. debate on the issue, two probable courses are foreseen: multipolarism and polycentrism. Should a multipolar order be implanted, it would mean that the main powers would conjugate their regional dominance with a matching weight on international relations resulting in an equilibrium in the world system. However, should the polycentrist trend prevail, the main powers would have to exercise their hegemony in their respective influence spheres resulting in an uneven status among them. How leadership will be exerted in each alternative is something to make out considering the factors traditionally involved in the formulation of U.S. international projection.

Once the above-mentioned matters—new globalization-oriented doctrine on U.S. national security, the diverse degrees of application of the global leadership and hegemony project, and the probable course of the trends imposed on the international relation system—could be duly clarified, the basis to predict the role and place of the Cuban-U.S. conflict within such matters could be laid. The result of such forecast would then enable to determine the contents of a Cuban security policy within a new world order.

The disappearance process of the socialist camp and the elimination of the East-West contradiction, the fastness and intensity of the latest technical and scientific progress, the formation of economic-commercial blocs, and the new strategies of transnational companies to reach a higher degree of globalization in world economy are some of the main facts that seem to explain the replacement of the relative importance of economic and politico-military factors regarding U.S. national security doctrine by the former.

Upon the disappearance of the U.S.S.R.—a military power and first bastion of an alternative social and political system to capitalism—the "dangers" to U.S. national security need to be redefined and relocated where the power of the nations really lies: in their economic potentialities.

U.S. economic potential is based on two axes. In the one hand, on its capacity to continue playing a given preponderant role worldwide before the economic power shown by the two other power "centers"—Germany and Japan. On the other hand, on its capacity to take the best possible advantage of the underdeveloped world as to have an ample and diversified economic rear guard to help it during the tough international competition the world will undoubtedly be involved in the near future.

Both axes of U.S. national security will involve attraction-repulsion maneuvers between the United States and the other pole. Achieving the common objectives of the centers regarding the underdeveloped world will imply harmonizing policies and collective approach to the problems. These may contribute to create rules, principles, and new-type institutions—or to modify the existing ones—in order to regulate the international economic and political relations in a new world order.

U.S. pretensions to stand over the remaining "centers" could bring about diverse frictions which would not only be expressed through contradictions and/or actions against the centers but also through the relations between the centers and the underdeveloped countries.

U.S. national security depends on its second axis. This consists of a multiphase and complex set of factors which, transcending the strictly economic field, drifts into others: the social field—demographic problems, migrations—; the technical and scientific field—incapacity of the countries to keep abreast of the technical and scientific breakthroughs, increase of the economic and technical and scientific gap—; and the institutional field—contradictions in the economic situation and other kind of problems among underdeveloped countries, and their capabilities to host the modernization of their societies through the creation of mechanisms enabling certain degree of social mobility.

Consequently, this axis of U.S. national security is likely to become a very controversial one. Together with the old angle of the North-South contradictions—hushed up under the East-West contradictions—the emergence of new problems, that complicate the relations between the "center" states and the underdeveloped world, is shaping up.

Inasmuch as some actions undertaken by the United States to obtain worldwide hegemony not only mean segregation for underdeveloped countries related to decision making and progressive priority reconsiderations of their burdensome problems but also U.S. stated pretension to openly intervene in the performance of the economies and societies of South nations by enforcing economic policies, among others, to be followed by underdeveloped nations, we will witness a period of important aggressions to the principles of sovereignty respect, self-determination, independence, and meddling in internal affairs.

In the international scene some hints indicate that the unipolarism enjoyed by U.S. leadership and hegemony is transitory too. The great number of opposing signs manifesting in the system of international relations are the determinants among which Cuban foreign policy might make the fundamentals of our revolutionary project—which are going through a definition process—valid and feasible both domestically and internationally.

Searching for a New Fundament for U.S. National Security Concept and Strategy

For the United States the end of the Cold War did not mean the triumph it had expected regarding the implantation of its uncontested hegemony. It was due to a number of internal and external processes that had started long before. These were consequence of the relative erosion of U.S. economic power as a result of the recovery of the remaining developed capitalist powers during the 1960s and the costs involved in the international leadership the United States has exercised since the end of the World War II in the context of its opposing the U.S.S.R.

The formulation in 1985 of the doctrine on removing the ideological angle from international relations—on the part of the U.S.S.R.—not only initiated a reevaluation of the U.S.S.R.-U.S. relations by the formulators and enforcers of U.S. foreign policy but also unchained a debate on the future of U.S. national security in all related levels.

Since 1987, just as a profound transformation of the international relation system started—a transformation that is still in progress—, a pungent discussion on U.S. political participation in the new world order began in U.S. political and academic circles. Since then the meaning for the United States of issues like interdependence of nation states, military security, and the challenge of the remaining economic powers—especially Japan— could be predicted.[61]

61. Refer to Kim R. Holmes, "Bush's New World Order: What's Wrong with this Picture?"*The Heritage Lectures*, no. 333, 1991; Harry M. Buchman, *U.S. Security in the Twenty-First Century* (Boulder, Colo.: Westview Press, 1987). In this study predictions requested by the General Research Program of the Institute for Defense Analysis, *American Security in an Interdependent World. A Collection of Papers Presented on the Atlantic Council's 1987 Annual Conference* (Laham: University Press of America, 1988). Among the authors whose papers are included in this volume is Zbigniew Brzezinski, former presidential counselor on national security affairs.

The end of the Cold War has consolidated the debate on the new bases for the security of the diverse nations and brought it to the forefront of world reality. It cannot be denied that all concerned agree upon the fact that economy will be the source for international influencing capacity of nation states in the near future.

Thus the nineties opened under multipolarism conditions that have been developing in the economic level. It consists of three main poles or centers led by the United States, Germany, and Japan—mostly referred to as The Triad in specialized literature. But the only superpower surviving the Cold War is only such in the strategic-military field. Although the United States keeps its politico-ideological influencing capacity over the rest of the capitalist powers—in spite of the fact that its leadership is not questioned— and its zone of influence in the Americas remains tightly under control, it faces considerable challenges from both the North and the South.

As a result of this, U.S. enjoyment of strategic-military unipolarity originates when such factors lose ground to the economic ones. It is not due to lack of armed conflicts in the international context, but rather because the challenges faced by the United States and the rest of the world cannot be solved from the perspective of military power.

The disappearance of the socialist camp and the dismembering of the U.S.S.R. not only put an end to the order of the international system which had prevailed for almost fifty years and had made it possible for the United States to consolidate its hegemony and leadership over a good part of the globe but also meant that U.S. political class—lacking the clear directions of bipolarity—is going through an identity crisis related to the role and place of the nation under the new conditions.

The national political consensus—which could be generated in favor of U.S. global projection in its fighting the nazi-fascist axis and was immediately transferred to stop communism after World War II—has definitively been broken once its bases—foreign threat and internal prosperity—crumbled.

One of the indexes to ascertain the profound commotion caused in the United States by the disappearance of the bipolar conflict after World War II is the lack of consensus on the interrelation between the domestic situation and U.S. international projection—the core issue of social worries—within the political and academic circles.

After almost half a century of internal consensus on the fundamentals of the national security conception —to stop communism and eventually make it fall back and its strategy—its interests and worldwide role—, U.S. academic and political circles and the media are facing the need to reconsider the principles which have led U.S. foreign policy during that period, and to redefine U.S. role and place in the world context. The goal of the debate on U.S. national security is to obtain consensus on foreign policy principles for the immediate future. This involve ideological, theoretical, and strategic steps to be undertaken in the world order in progress.

Forced to restore the international relations according to the global changes that were taking place and facing difficult domestic problems derived from a relative loss of economic competitiveness to other capitalist powers, the United States is to redefine its national priorities.

The collapse of the national security paradigm that dominated the thought of U.S. foreign policymakers along the Cold-War historical period, the lack of consensus on the nature of the contemporary world, the uncertainty in regard to the challenges the United States will face in future decades, the political imperative of revamping the country, the need to destine resources for domestic urgencies, and public pressures for old and new beyond-frontiers commitments to be established are the main directions of the debate on the best way to guarantee national security.

The event of a debate on the new national security strategy within the U.S. society does not mean of course that there is a total lack of concern on the part of the fields involved in the exercise of U.S. foreign policy. The Clinton administration—the first one to govern the only surviving superpower after the Cold War—has shown confusion and theoretical void to face the new international challenges when "the enemy" is no longer. Although the new topics and issues upon which the United States will have to base its relations with the rest of the world have been introduced in the rhetoric, the political debate continues to be polarized and, in practice, the lack of coherence distinguishing the struggle among diverging thought trends is evident.

At least in the speeches so far delivered, the current U.S. president has stated his interest that the national security strategy to be formed has a multilateral orientation. Despite the Clinton administration is still ambiguous when it comes to the point of specifying its priorities on national security, it cannot be denied that the governing team and its counselors show a political and intellectual proneness to define the U.S. democracy-associated interest and to establish a suitable multilateral ambit for the economic, strategic and military future. This differs from the typically-realistic Republican position that emphasizes power balance.[62]

The development of this trend is limited by two of the more debated subjects between multilateralists and segregationists: economic security and military security.

62. Creating the Economic Security Council; stressing economic, technological, and social development as a source to exercise leadership and hegemony; and showing an intense activity to eliminate nuclear weapons.

The debate is not restricted to the old segregationist and "internationalist" trends, but even among those who favor an active participation in international affairs discuss whether the efforts should be focused on the Asia-Pacific area—because it shows the highest economic dynamism in the world, and involves the most important challenges for the United States which are due not only to the presence of Japan and the so-called tigers but also to the endeavors of China that could become a superpower next century— or on Europe—as the "Atlantists" state—where the key to maintaining U.S. supremacy lies.

The end of the Cold War has aided interdependence, intensification in global economy. But the United States has just finished a period of confronting the USSR, and it meant an injury to U.S. economic interests—thus it paid for its reaching an alliance with Europe and Japan against the enemy. The lack of bipolar opposition has freed the United States from that commitment, and now it needs to boost its economic interests in spite of the fact that it will generate tensions with its traditional allies considering the present state of affairs in the world.

But the debate is not only concerned with the areas the United States should direct its efforts to and center its attention on. The discussion also shows the struggle between internal forces, which oppose or help the economic globalization process due to its implication for U.S. society, and the role the United States is to play as a world power.

Furthermore it must be taken into account that for the last fifty years U.S. policy has showed ally-commitment as its main feature in spite of the fact that it depended on them to orchestrate actions to stop communism or to make it fall back.

The existing U.S. debate—whose background is the ways and means to enable the United States to enjoy permanent and uncontested leadership and global hegemony in the future world order—shows that the globalization design the capitalist power centers are conforming, is a phenomenon which involves not only the opposing North-South interests but also the fundamentals for the emergence of new forms of interpower conflict.

Both the debate and the events clearly indicate that the relations with the remaining powers is the most relevant challenge to be faced by the United States in its condition of center-country. Thus, should we stick to the fact that—as far as interdependence among nations is concerned—the United States, like the other central countries, concentrates its interest on intra-North relations, our previous statements regarding South *segregation* and *exclusion* from the globalization project, and lack of interest to reach some degree of harmony in North-South relations are confirmed.

It is therefore understandable that U.S. thought on current foreign policy struggles between the need to attain final consolidation of unipolarism—however transitory—resulting from the disappearance of bipolarism, and the urge to share with its fellow-powers the cost of maintaining a world order profitable to all.

According to such imperatives, one of the intensively-questioned issues is whether the United States is really powerful to keep on playing the role and occupying the place it has defined for itself in the system of international relations. Therefore the most diverse sectors of U.S. society are busy trying to determine whether the United States is *declining* or not.

A relevant feature of the debate studied hereon is the emotional context which it takes place in. Regardless who agrees to the notion that U.S. society is declining, it cannot be denied that the recurring discussion of the issue shows at least a profound doubt of U.S. internal and international real power. The participants in the debate are aligned on two sides—the ones who are concerned with the contribution of the South to U.S. economic recovery, and the ones who consider intercenter relations to be the key element to U.S. economic leadership.

Ronald W. Roskens, administrator of the International Development Agency, stated before the Committee on Foreign Affairs of the U.S. House of Representatives that the relevance of the Third World market for U.S. economy performance made it necessary to aid the growth and development of underdeveloped nations as a way of increasing national security. Expanding such markets is the target of the Agency's aid programs in the belief that "poor peoples mean poor consumers."[63] This statement implicitly recognizes that globalization cannot be achieved ignoring a North-South relation that assures certain degree of harmony in its development. However, the legitimacy of the subordinate role of the South—just a market place where North productions are realized—relative to the North is not questioned.

The issue of U.S. declining power was subject to profound analysis in a seminar under the auspices of the Congressional Research Service by request of the Subcommittee on International Economic Policy and Trade of the House Committee on Foreign Affairs which was interested in answering questions like: Is U.S. power declining? Is it the moment when another country will be the leader of the next century or is it a transition period? Can power be defined by automobile-building capacity, by computer-selling level, by doctorate-scholarship granted, by wars won?[64]

63. House of Representatives, *The Future of U.S. Foreign Policy in the Post-Cold War Era. Hearings before the Committee on Foreign Affairs*, 102d Cong., 2d sess., February 6, 19 and 20; March 5 and 24, and April 30, 1992 (Washington D.C.: U.S. Government Printing Office, 1992).

64. *U.S. Power in a Changing World. Proceedings of a Seminar Held by the Congressional Research Service. November 19-20, 1989.* Re-

The main concerns on U.S. current situation to face the developing process of globalization may be summed up from the matters discussed by government officers, congressmen, and academicians who attended the above-mentioned seminar. These concerns involve:

1. National power in a changing world,
2. The economic dimension of power,
3. The technological dimension of power,
4. The military dimension of power,
5. Maintaining U.S. influence.

The discussion of the last item on the list showed in all its magnitude U.S. profound concern about what the challenge of the Japanese economic, and technical and scientific potential means. It also showed that the issue of the politico-economic implications related to whether military reductions should be effected or not is at a crossroad.[65]

A debate on foreign policy has always been a tradition in U.S. thought. A nation like the United States —founded on the belief that it was a counterpattern for late-18th century European society, which excluded the chance of a high degree of involvement on international problems—made the controversy on its participation in world affairs one of the characteristics of the formation process of its foreign policy.

This feature deepened as foreign policy turned into a policy for leadership exercise. During the Cold War era geopoliticians, realists, and liberal internationalists dived into an intense debate on the appropriate means to reach the goals set by U.S. interests. So the structuring period of the Cold War world order was the ideal con-

port prepared for the Subcommittee on International Economic Policy and Trade of the Committee on Foreign Affairs, U.S. House of Representatives, by the Congressional Research Service Library of Congress Washington D.C.: U.S. Government Printing Office, 1990).
65. Ibid, 93-131.

text in which the Founding Fathers' principles about world-wide responsibility, the theoretical fundamentals which developed in the late 19th century and the imperatives of an expanding imperialist nation crystalized. In brief, consensus on the national security conception after World War II made the determination of the corresponding strategy the principal task. Since then, a definition of a national interest that stops at nothing, prevails.

Hence, the end of the Cold War—once the consensus on national security conception was broken—has forced the diverse sectors involved in forming U.S. foreign policy to create a new consensus from the identification of the fundamentals of a security conception. This should enable to seek the suitable strategy under the present circumstances. It explains why the two main directions of the debate refer to delimiting *the nature of the future international system* to be and U.S. role once such system is operative.

As we shall be able to examine hereinafter, the debate around national security conception in the world order to be not only refers to the doctrinal fundamentals to build it on—plus its strategical and tactical aspects—but also to the efficiency of the analytical models so far employed.[66]

For that cause, the profound transformation the international relation system is undergoing determines that such issues like the definition of national interest, the type of alliances to be formed, the usefulness of employing military force, and the need to establish an in-

66. Refer to Richard Rosecrance and Arthur A. Stein, eds., *The Domestic Bases of Grand Strategy* (New York: Cornell University Press, 1993; Mark A. Brawley, *Liberal Leadership: Great Powers and Their Challenges in Peace and War* (New York: Cornell University Press, 1993; and Robert H. Jackson and Alan James, *States in a Changing World: A Contemporary Analysis* (New York: Oxford University Press, 1993).

dustrial policy acquire first-degree relevance. Among them, the role of technological development in the new economic trends and its influence upon the performance or disappearance of national boundaries occupy an outstanding place.

On such a relevant matter the fallacy of the central countries—the United States among them—stands out. During the discussions on *the new content of a nation state*, the defense of U.S. boundaries does not seem to be contradictory—whatever its implications in terms of restricting other countries' actions regarding trade, investments, migrations, etcetera—to the increasingly spread consideration that the states and boundaries of South countries should disappear on behalf of the benefits of interdependence.

Among those who advocate the criterion of the disappearance of the boundaries and consequently of the nation states is Robert Reich, labor secretary of the Clinton administration. He defines the matter as follows: "National productions and technologies shall disappear, national corporations and industries shall disappear, i.e., national economies shall no longer exist."[67]

Contrary to Reich's argument is the one that broaches the acceptance that the Cold War stagnate old nationalisms. While the latter have made a dramatic come back, they are less relevant than the economic rivalries that distinguished the world between the two world wars. Therefore the return to geopolitic and economic rivalry patterns is the cause for leaving the nature of the role of the nation state on the international arena unchanged. The great historic circles caused by compe-

67. Robert Reich, *The World of Nations: Preparing Ourselves for the 21st Century Capitalism* (New York: Alfred A. Knopf, n.d..), 3. Quoted in Ronald D. Amus's work.

tition or conflicts between states still exist despite Francis Fukuyama's affirmation that we have arrived at the end of History.[68]

Authors like Lester Thurow consider that in the next fifty years the world will be dominated by the fight among Japan, Europe, and the United States for the economic competitive leadership and the attempt to make their respective capitalism models prevail.[69]

Other contribution to this line of thought is made by Edward N. Luttwak who stated that in 1945 the world was arranged by the existence of two military superpowers—the United States and the Soviet Union—but one of them—the United States—happened to be an economic superpower as well. Contrary to the situation at that time, the end of the Cold War shows one military superpower—the United States—and three economic superpowers—Germany, Japan, and the United States. So the author considers that there is a transit from geopolitics to geoeconomics in terms of conceptualizing the context definition to identify nation-states' interests. The relevance of making conclusions on this matter lies in the identification of the U.S. industrial policy.

The same happens with the subject of the definition of the ideal tool to drive the relations among the more powerful nation states. While the military confrontation prevailing during the Cold War era made it necessary to

68. Ronald D. Asmus, *The New U.S. Strategic Debate. Prepared for the United States Army* (Santa Monica, Calif.: RAND, 1993), 9. In our research report we follow the patterns outlined by Ronald Asmus in his study regarding the debate on national-security strategy under the paragraph titled "Looking for U.S. role and place in the future system of international relations. Identifying the strategy." Further development of the research work we have started will include other studies, statements, and theses referred to by Asmus.

69. Lester Thurow, *Head to Head; The Coming Economic Battle among Japan, Europe and America* (New York: William Morrow and Co., 1992), 23. Quoted in Asmus, op cit., 10.

resort to pacific coexistence, in the world under configuration pacific coexistence is to be replaced by economic coexistence. Therefore, for those who advocate the criterion of the preeminence of economic development as power source for a given nation, multilateralism will become the tool to achieve economic coexistence.[70]

The debate is not restricted to create a consensus within the postmodern ideotheoretical realm because the "old way of thinking" that led to the Cold War once World War II ended is not dead. It survives in the attempts to maintain and to spread NATO to the East—this being a strategic guarantee if power rearrangement in Europe is effected without U.S. participation and the economic competition with the allies results unfavorable for U.S. leadership positions. According to Warren Christopher, former secretary of state of the Clinton administration—the United States must project its influence from its Atlantic dimension.[71]

The strategic-military and security concerns keep on holding a preponderant place in U.S. relations with Europe, where—according to an article by Senator Robert Dole in *Foreign Policy* magazine[72]—preventing a single power to become dominant continues to be a priority for the United States, and where there are still vital interests related to the nuclear arsenal of the former USSR and the probability of a rebirth of Russian expansionist nationalism.

Since Mijail Gorbachev—former secretary-general of the U.S.S.R. Communist Party—made a statement on the need to remove ideological issues from interna-

70. Edward N. Luttwak, "From Geopolitics to Geoeconomics: Logic of Conflict, Grammar of Commerce," *The National Interest* (Summer 1990), 17-23. Quoted in Asmus, op. cit., 11.

71. Refer to Warren Christopher, "America's Leadership, America's Opportunity," *Foreign Policy,* 98 (Spring 1995), 19.

72. Robert Dole, "Shaping America's Global Future," *Foreign Policy* 98 (Spring 1995), 29-43.

lations, in the United States an ever-encreasing debate on *national interest redefinition* especially focused on Asian development—mainly that of Japan—, was initiated.[73]

As far as the considerations of the general context to define national interest is concerned, they follow the two main lines of U.S. traditional thought on the matter: *realism* and *internationalism*.

Realists—Henry Kissinger being one of its most distinguished exponents—still consider that the supreme interest of the nation is achieving power balance. While during the Cold War era realists believed that the essential question was to establish a proper power balance between the United States and the U.S.S.R., today, in the post-Cold War era, they state that the question is maintaining U.S. sovereignty, reaching a flexible security strategy, and preventing the emergence of a new hegemony opposed to the U.S.[74]

The rather consensual attitude of realists on the principles that should guide the definition of national interest does not exclude putting their theoretical models under reconsideration. The limits and possibilities of the theoretical constructions on which realism (*realpolitik*) has based itself are emphasized on critic studies on the subject.[75]

Internationalists—rooted on Woodrow Wilson's thought—stress the role of democracy and law as guarantors to

73. U.S. Power in a Changing World. Proceedings of a seminar held by the Congressional Research Service - November 19-20, 1989. Report prepared for the Subcommittee on International Economic Policy and Trade of the Committee on Foreign Affairs, U.S. House of Representatives, by the Congressional Research Service Library of Congress, U.S. Government Printing Office, Washington D.C., 1990.

74. Asmus, op. cit., 13.

75. For instance, Frank W. Wayman and Paul F. Diehl, *Reconstructing Realpolitik* (The University of Michigan Press, 1994).

define national interests and consequently national security. Expanding democracy, spreading multilateral and cooperation institutions, and building up a wider and more effective system of collective security in a changing and increasingly dependent world are the pillars which national interests are to be erected upon.[76]

Segregationism, unilateralism, multilateralism, and defense of collective security are the four main lines of U.S. thought regarding the national security strategy which should guide the exercise of its foreign policy. The attention of those four lines of thought is focused on the efforts to try to delimit *the role and place of the United States in the future international system*.[77]

Segregationists are based on the imperative need for internal strengthening and maintaining strategic independence as opposed to the partisans of involvement in international affairs, whose profit is marginal and which erodes national well-being and prosperity. According to this current, the defense of U.S. national interests requires quitting present alliances because they correspond to an international state of affairs no longer existing. Segregationists propose as their goals to achieve global stability, and a new world order in which democracy becomes a new pillar of national security strategy.

In keeping with this, segregationists' priority lies in maintaining the existing bonds with the regions from which the United States obtains raw materials and to which the United States can market its production and make investments in. The economic supremacy as core of national security conception and strategy is stated again.

Unilateralists, on their part, consider that the key purpose of the national security strategy is for the United

76. Asmus, op. cit., 15.
77. Asmus, op. cit., 21-39.

States to maintain its post-Cold War advantages and to prevent the emergence of new strategic dangers. Although they agree with segregationists on the need to preserve the strategic independence, they give special force to maintain global interests.

As they believe that collective security and multilateral organizations are not efficient to guarantee an effective performance of the international security system, they trust that, if the United States exactly define its vital issues of interest, it may be able to maintain its strategic independence and a strong capability to answer to a potential crisis.

Other unilateralist strategic objectives are to keep strong bonds with the main actors of the international system, which will enable to attain a power balance in important regions while preventing the emergence of new hegemonies within them. On that ground, the cases of Germany and Japan in Europe and Asia, respectively, should be taken care of.

Multilateralism flag-bearers consider that interdependence is the basis of an international policy oriented to attain democratization and globalization of politics and economy. U.S. security and well-being assume the adoption of "a new kind of internationalism" which must be erected upon multilateral institutions assuring cooperation to reach higher goals. Skeptics of UN efficiency recommend the creation of a "western global caucus" in which the United States is no longer afraid of European and Japanese presence because they should be stimulated to assume a more important role relative to guaranteeing international security. U.S. relevant position in the international relation system allows its being able to outline the key elements of a new world order.

The return to the Wilsonian principles makes the partisans of a national security strategy consider justice and law enforcement the directives to attain *collective security*. While they are opposed to the use of force, they do not avoid it when necessary to preserving collective security.

U.S. privileged position in the United Nations Security Council should be taken advantage of to put an end to the stagnation caused by the Cold War within that organization. The proposal of those in favor of collective security considers that the fact that the United States occupies and retains a world leadership position does not mean it becomes an international guardian. The aim is to achieve a presence in world problems capable of maintaining the leadership that preserves the suitable world order for U.S. national security at a bearable cost.

The existence of four lines of thought in the complex process of searching for a new national security strategy for the United States does not imply that the one put into force excludes the rest. On the contrary, it might be predicted that a sort of coalition could be formed among them as all four recognize that the United States deserves a leadership and hegemony role in the new world order under development.

The United States is opposed to a concertation with the remaining capitalist powers and somehow fears its becoming subject to multilateral mechanisms which might hinder its proneness to undertake unilateral actions. This is exemplified by U.S. ambiguous relation with the United Nations and its position before GATT and its successor, the World Trade Organization.

The fact that U.S. politics consistently claims for economic issues to be negotiated internationally does not mean it is in a position to achieve it. Such a situation may decrease support to multilateral international activity and strengthen the positions of segregationists and unilateralists within society.

In the same way the United States, Europe and Japan are moving around the international arena as equals and defending the same interests, the bonds that used to agglutinate their behavior—facing communism—have broken.

The other great challenge faced by a multilateral position is the question of military security. The poles of debate are formed around the answer to "How much is minimum enough to assure military security?"—which replaced "How much is enough?," formulated during the Cold War era. The difficulties to give a right answer that favors one of the opposing positions derive from the fact that some consider that the United States cannot presently define the dangers it might encounter while reality shows the nation enjoys an unprecedented military security.

Therefore, the military security strategy must look to preserving alliances and maintaining the prevailing regional stability.[78] This is the position that gives continuity to the base-force policy advocated by the former president George Bush and his predecessor.

The importance still accorded to U.S. military capacity to face potential challenges—an issue that also worries the remaining capitalist central countries— clearly shows that forcing competition in the economy field will not progress rapidly. To solve those problems of a South-coming obstruction of globalization—whose fundamentals are being defined by the North—the use of military force is not excluded. But the question of the military capacity of the powers could also indicate that to solve potential rivalries among them, the use of force might turn out to be a useful resource.

78. Dick Cheney, former secretary of defense of the Clinton administration, is an example of such a position. Refer to Department of Defense, *Defense Strategy for the 1990s: The Regional Defense Strategy*, Washington, January 1993, pp. 8-9. Quoted in Asmus, op.cit., 33.

There are those however who believe in the need to elaborate alternatives to the use of military force according to the events, i.e., the cases of Iraq and Panama. But they cannot answer the question about the implications of this kind of actions on U.S. relations with its allies.[79]

In spite of the opposing positions, there is a consensual domain when it comes to recognizing the need to consider the political and military consequences of a given military-security strategy; that is, if the defense-expense cuts are likely to affect the politico-economic goals of the nation; if a certain military-security strategy may guarantee or not the geopolitic stability in those zones and regions where U.S. presence has traditionally been strong; as well as the analytical instruments to measure and to evaluate the potential risks to be faced by U.S. military-security strategy.[80]

The conviction that national security strategy must be oriented to consolidate collective security through worldwide diffusion of democracy and the role of law on international relations—thus the emphasis on the military angle would be decreased—seems to express the line of thought of the Democratic Party stated by the candidates to the presidency with slogans like "America First" and "Come Home America" in the 1992 electoral campaign. That could be the basis for stating that President Clinton is a foreign-policy multilateralist but a military segregationist.

Another issue open to debate is U.S. participation in multilateral military operations.

79. Lee H. Hamilton, "A Democrat Looks at Foreign Policy," *Foreign Affair* (Summer 1992), 30-51. Quoted in Asmus, op. cit., 36.
80. U.S. Power in a Changing World. Proceedings of a seminar held by the Congressional Research Service. November 19-20, 1989. Report prepared for the Subcommittee on International Economic Policy and Trade of the Committee on Foreign Affairs, U.S. House of Representatives, by the Congressional Research Service Library of Congress, U.S. Government Printing Office, Washington D.C., 1990, pp. 67 ff.

Public opinion—however little consulted in the future of national security and foreign policy compared to previous moments in U.S. history—seems to be totally in favor of an internal-external balance, and emphasizes on the economic and political problems of the future model of national security. Regarding military-security strategy, public opinion has veered its attention to multilateralist positions.[81]

The William Clinton Administration Performance

THE UNITED STATES AND ITS ALLIES

The relations between the United States and its allies in the extinct East-West conflict are increasingly antagonistic and complementary due to their featuring a high degree of interdependence—as befitting a globalized world economy in which the main mergers and alliances are made among U.S., European, and Japanese corporations.

Preserving whatever form of U.S. leadership depends on restructuring the alliance system agreed upon during the Cold War context. Such system however will not be able to lie in U.S. "nuclear umbrella" as it did before, but will necessarily involve in politico-economic contents. These must guarantee for the United States to maintain its influence on diverse areas of the planet at a time in which there is a rush to form regional commercial blocks, and regional organizations are strengthened.

Since the beginning, the first Clinton administration maintained contradictions with its West European allies on the security structures in the region and the armed

81. "The Emerging World Order, Americans Talk Security Issues," Survey no. 16. Quoted in Asmus, op. cit., 95.

conflict in former Yugoslavia to which the end of the "honeymoon" with Russia due to the same reasons may be added.

This fact has manifested both in bilateral ambits and in multilateral ones, and has caused the failure of the summit of the Conference on Security and Cooperation in Europe (CSCE) held in December 1994, and the high-level contacts made between U.S. and Russian representatives all along 1995 to prepare President Clinton's visit to Russia on the 50th Anniversary of the Victory over Nazism.

Russia could but consider the extension of NATO membership to former signatories of the Warsaw Pact as a maneuver to isolate it in the European theater, and to militarily fence its frontiers over. Such a U.S. move has a certain degree of consensus among the European powers—except for France, which outstandingly considers a hurried-up spread of NATO or the West European Union (an exclusively European military organization) could bring about a disrupting effect on the continent. To counterbalance this maneuver, Russia had propitiated for the CSCE to broaden its scope—restricted to preventive-diplomacy activities since it was created back in 1975—and made it assume a brand-new role that would turn it into a first-level mechanism to solve East European and Central European conflicts.

The United States has stated that enlarging the military alliance into a pan-European security structure continued to be a supreme objective and that no formula would be able to lessen it—not even the newly born Association for Peace.

The Bosnian conflict was the main touchstone between the United States and NATO allies, and a friction item in Russian-U.S. relations.

The gap between Russia and the United States was prone to broaden up during 1995. The meeting between the foreign-policy heads of both countries—Kosiriev and

Christopher—held in Geneva, and the one between the defense heads—Grachov and Perry—, intended to pave the way for a Yeltsin-Clinton summit, were unable to close it. And the presidential meeting opened among unsatisfactions and mutual recriminations, worsened by the military option undertaken by Russia against Chechenia, and Russian decision to sell nuclear reactors to Iran.

Beyond the issues of discord, the European problems the United States is opposed to, express latent tensions in the international context which invalidate U.S. pretensions to implant its unrestricted supremacy in the Old Continent once the Cold War is over. It is so because the United States does not recognize the variety of interests competing for power redefinition and redistribution in that area—which had been divided into two hostile fields for almost half a century, and where U.S. presence has lost economic and political meaning. However U.S. presence continues playing a significant ideological and strategic-military role.

The summit of the Asia-Pacific Economic Conference (APEC), held in Bogor, near Jakarta, Indonesia, on November 14-15, 1994, was a true example of U.S. interest in the Asian region—where 40% of the world trade is concentrated, and where the United States faces the greatest economic challenges, introduced not only by Japan and China but also by the famous new first- and second-generation industrialized nations.

The excellent growth rates shown by most countries in the area and the creation of the World Trade Organization—which was to replace GATT since January 1, 1995—made that APEC's second meeting specially meaningful for the United States, interested in keeping the Asian gates opened to U.S. trade. It was due to the fact that the Asian members' GDP totalled 13 billion dollars—almost half the world's GDP.

It must be noticed that the United States centered its efforts on achieving for the Asia-Pacific area to be declared a free-trade zone by 2020 without stressing on such conditions as democracy, human-rights respect, and labor issues that distinguish its relations with underdeveloped countries.

Quite different is U.S. projection relative to the region where it still exerts strong control and influence, and where it is turning to in search of the elements that could enable it to restructure its hegemony and to project its world leadership under the new international conditions.

LATIN AMERICA—CURRENT POLITICS. HEMISPHERIC DIVERGENCES

The realities of competition in the globalization process have encouraged increased concern about the forgotten and unheeded regions of Latin America and the Caribbean. In spite of their being U.S. immediate sphere of influence and the platform from which the United States projects its hegemony and leadership, they have always occupied a subordinate place in U.S. priorities.

Then the criterion that the hemisphere might become the stronghold for future U.S. power started to push its way through. Such power gain could become effective via a greater integration of Latin-American economies subject to U.S. needs—which results in a novelty, given the legendary underestimation and lack of attention the powerful neighbor has shown toward its "lesser partners" in the region, which always has been the pivot, the military engine and the prism of its strategic security interests with a low economic profile.[82]

82. Lars Shoultz, "Inter-American Security: The Changing Perception of U.S. Policy Makers." Paper prepared for the meeting of the LASA Work Group on Security in the Caribbean, April 26-28, 1990.

Such an interest in its continental neighbors is not at all a consensual issue in U.S. foreign policy, but it does have concrete implementation examples in the region, like the Initiative for the Americas, the extension of the North American Free Trade Agreement to Chile and other countries, and the Summit of the Americas held late 1994. During the summit, a statement on the creation of a hemispheric free-trade zone was put forward. It is indeed part of U.S. change regarding security conceptions and foreign-menace perceptions. The United States always based its relations with neighbours on an extracontinental-power-refraining strategy—be they with the Holly Alliance in the last century, or with the USSR during the Cold War.

Since the 1980s, as communism refraining lost credibility as a consensus-forming element to interventionism in Latin America and the Caribbean, the United States started to transfer the ideas on national-security menace to nontraditional subjects like narcotraffic, terrorism, emigration, and environmental pollution.

While the geopolitics logistics considers the hemisphere as U.S. long-abandoned and unheeded "backyard," under the geoeconomics light it gains fresh relevance for the United States at a time its economic competitiveness depends—for the most part—on its successful participation in the globalization process, which requires the creation of a continental megamarket from Alaska to Patagonia.[83]

But the United States is not after merely economic objectives in the region. It is not even after mainly economic objectives as demonstrated by the low degree of

83. Xabier Gorostiaga, "América Latina frente a los desafíos globales," in *Estado, nuevo orden económico y democracia en América Latina* (Caracas: Alas-CEA, Editorial Nueva Sociedad, 1992), 53-75.

relevance given to extending NAFTA to other countries of the continent—a process that does not enjoy a solid consensus within the United States, but is the main attraction for Latin-American elites.

Rebuilding U.S. hegemonic foundations in its sphere of immediate influence demands farther-reaching formulas to stabilize the area. These must surpass the "magic" formula of free trade and investment, and are directly related to the installation of a society model based on the values and institutions of the so-called representative democracy.

Hence, U.S. projection south of its borders involves a number of conditions which—as a whole—form a new type of interventionism in the region in order to homogenize it to U.S. global interests.

Achieving economic symmetry must be escorted by the creation of some conditions within underdeveloped societies enabling certain modicum of stability. One of such conditions is generalizing the conservative-democracy model, which emphasizes such formal elements as free elections and multipartism, but disregards pluriparticipation in the political-power structures.

The stabilizing formula of market economy and representative democracy also comprises other elements like the so-called "good governance," constitutional amendments to reduce state power, the reform of the judicial systems, decreasing and reorienting the armed forces, and—at a regional level—strengthening the inter-American system and making it assimilate new economic, political, and military contents.

These are considered key elements in a meddling design aimed at weakening and reducing all state roles in favor of economic globalization. This also requires certain conditions of political and social stability, and eliminating all obstacles to free action of transnational capital.

In fact, it means transferring the American Way of Life to Latin-American societies by assimilating U.S. values and political practices. Such a process progressively erases the features of their national identities.

Obviously there is a generalized consensus among Latin American political elites on this project coming from the center. It manifests in the stronger economies of the region. These economies aim at belonging to the select group of industrialized nations—"The First World"—through the market magic, where free trade is considered the main development tool in the planet.

In the referred to bibliography—which covers the generalities of the debate on U.S. security doctrine and strategy for the new world order—there are numerous references to the challenges to U.S. power Japan and Europe mean from the most diverse angles. The opposite is true for Latin America, despite the importance it has historically had for the international projection of U.S. interests.

As it became obvious that a new world order was emerging, the first problem discussed—from a chronological point of view—about the future of U.S.-Latin-American relations was the employment of military intervention. Although U.S. military intervention in Latin America is a phenomenon prior to the Cold War, the World Peace Foundation has planned to make a research on cooperation in the future system of inter-American security. The research will focus on determining whether the end of the Cold War might have broken the cycle of insecurity and fear underlying inter-American relations resulting from U.S., use of the military intervention against its neighboring republics in the southern part of the continent.[84]

An analysis of this nature anticipated the need to reconsider the traditional military element as basis for hemispheric security. Likewise it presented evidence of the fact that many statements regarding the regional security system had been created as a consequence of the Cold War and so they were just manipulations. The discussion on the use of military intervention on the part of the United States showed the alarm this kind of action awakened if it continues in a new world order without bipolar struggle.

A study made by the Woodrow Wilson Center in 1992[85] recognizes that the Inter-American Security System created in 1947-1948 failed because it was based on principles—systematically disregarded—the of nonintervention and collective security. That system helped U.S. extra-hemispheric interests and put aside agreements on subregional needs.

For Latin America the system acted as a common front against the danger involved in the expansion of the objectives of a European power—the Soviet Union. Participating together with the United States in communism refraining in the area aided the small countries to count on U.S. protection in case of an aggression from their big neighbors, while big states wanted U.S. support in their disputes with their neighbors. But U.S. recurrent use of military intervention against Latin-American nations questioned the real existence of a security system looking after the interests of the region.

---

84. Refer to Richard J. Bloomfield and Gregory Treverton, eds., *Alternative to Intervention: A New U.S.-Latin-American Security Relationship*. (Boulder, Colo.: Lynne Rienner Publishers, Inc., 1990).

85. Refer to Nina Serafino, "U.S. Security for Latin America and the Caribbean: Current Situation and Prospects," and Augusto Vargas, "Workshop Introduction," in *Redefining National Security in Latin America: Workshop Report*, Woodrow Wilson Center, November 16-17, 1992. (The Latin-American Program, no. 204.)

One of the most valuable conclusions on the future of security in the American continent commented on the study is the need to establish new-type bonds between Latin America and the United States. These bonds should be suitable to redesign the inter-American security system as a hemispheric forum for interchange and cooperation. Such a forum would differ from the existing one—whose character is that of a continental military alliance[86] in which the key regional issue (economic integration) only involves some Latin-American countries.

The other important conclusion is the need to overcome the prevailing contradiction between the two elements of the system through an effective mediation as to avoid the present state of affairs. So far one of the elements—the United States—arrogates the right to act single-handedly or in alliance against any of the members.[87]

The Cold War finished, the question of the economic fate of nation states is also a pressing concern for Latin-American countries. However the consensus around the preponderant role of the United States with an undisputed hegemony in the region has led the researchers on the subject to consider that, in the new world order, the security interests of Latin America will continue to be a function of the global U.S. interests and, consequently, a critical component of the regional security.

The state of unipolar power enjoyed by the United States is considered one of the obstacles to attain an inter-American security system in which the agreement on the interests of the parties is the basis for its existence.[88]

That is the cause for the essential disagreement between the Latin-American and the U.S. agendas on the restructuration of the regional security system. While the most important question for the United States is to avoid the emergence of a new hegemony in the region, for

86. Ibid., 34.
87. Ibid., 42.
88. Augusto Vargas, op. cit.

Latin America the core of its security interests is the issue of economic integration as the way to solve the
structural problems suffered by its economy, for they are
the only ones capable of offering a solid foundation for
the stability of their societies.[89]

Other differences lie in the way each of the parties
tries to solve matters affecting their respective
securities. Although both the United States and most
Latin-American countries are interested in eradicating
the noxious effects of narcotraffic, their respective
points of view are different. The United States is interested in controlling drug distribution and consumption
within its territory. But the problem becomes a complex
one for Latin America because U.S. cooperation is only
available for repression through the use of military
force.[90] Drug traffic continues to be a security concern
for the present Administration rather from a global
perspective than from a regional one focused on
narcotraffic prohibition.

The power balance between the armed forces and
the civil power in Latin-American nations is another security issue. U.S. and Latin-American interests again dis-
agree. The use of military power in the international
projection of a nation is a matter that precedes by far the
Cold War. It is not casual then that the U.S. debate on
military security shows such a relevance. In terms of U.S.

89. The outcome of the Summit of the Americas held in December 1994 showed the divorce of the priorities of the North and the
South in the hemisphere. While from the U.S. point of view the Summit
should aid to articulate hemispheric relations to face the challenges of
the formation of great economic blocks, from the Latin American leaders' angle the issues to solve were trade and investment growth, integration to a free-trade agreement with the United States, and the
elimination of poverty. But the passivity governing U.S. policy toward
Latin America only allowed for a pact on development and prosperity
based on democracy, free trade, and sustainable development as to
reach a free-trade zone by 2005. Refer to Luis René Fernández Tabío,
"La Cumbre de las Américas: ¿una nueva política para América
Latina?". Typescript.
90. Augusto Vargas, op. cit.

relations with Latin America, U.S. military presence in the region has not been questioned. The compliance with the Treaty of the Panama Canal would be never discussed if it were not for Latin America.

Armory, training, and budget of the armed forces is an issue considered as part of regional political stability. But the United States shows no interest in either reducing its military presence in the area, or helping model the size and function of Latin-American armies so they match the requirements for a good performance of democratic regimes.[91]

The issue of environmental deterioration seems to be another subject in which the differences between the Latin-American and the U.S. angles will make it hardly probable to reach an agreement on the efforts to approach it as an element of regional security.

On the University of San Diego, California, conference report on security redefinition in the regional context and the possible emergence of a new security structure in the area, it is affirmed that the Clinton administration has a narrow and ambiguous sight. The report states that the target of the inter-American relations should be to look for a "participative agenda" about one of the regional issues as to show there is a "community of democracies."[92]

Likewise Les Aspin, former secretary of defense, declared that the challenges to be faced by the United States are the regional conflicts, the proliferation of nuclear weapons, and the failures of political reforms and of the inclusion of economy as part of the security interests among the powers.

Regardless the debate on military security that is taking place in the United States, political practice shows

91. Francisco Rojas, "From War to Integration: Democratic Transition and Security Issues," in *Redefining National Security*; Shawn Butter, "Regional Security after the Cold War. Conference Report," *Working Papers*, no. 4 (November 1993), ed. by the Center for Iberian and Latin-American Studies (CILAS), 1993.

92. Butter, op. cit.

that the goal of maintaining and fostering military superiority is still present. In 1992 the Joint General Staff adjusted the military strategy to be ready to carry out politico-military actions consisting of increasing the means to boost U.S. advantages internationally.[93]

Finally, it is evident that in the Clinton administration policy toward Latin-America NAFTA and the OAS will offer room for just partial cooperation with Latin-American countries, which results from the disproportionate weight of the United States in the region. It allows the unilateral development of U.S. security objectives in the area without having to consider the regional ones.

Summing up, it is highly improbable that the new world order under formation is the scenario where Latin American and, of course, Caribbean countries will be able to establish both their security and the regional security based on the defense of their interests. Therefore, the principle of geopolitics will continue to have a decisive influence on inter-American relations. It would be worthwhile dedicating efforts to study the possibility of a world order in which geopolitics would keep on ruling the relations between the powers and their influence areas while geoeconomics would act as governing principle of the relations among highly industrialized countries.

The Summit of the Americas which gathered the heads of state of the Western Hemisphere—which had not been convoked by the United States since 1967—was inscribed precisely in this context. Furthermore, in the current U.S. and international situation the main purposes of the Summit were to settle the basis for a fresh relation with the region. It places the North-South problem under a different angle that enables the Latin-American and Caribbean underdeveloped countries to share a basic consensus with the United States on the need to integrate their economies. However the agenda had been arranged according to the terms de-

93. Ibid.

fined by the northern power and under unfavorable conditions.[94]

Nonetheless, the "modernization" of Latin-American economies according to the neoliberal paradigm—in which the market logic would take care of eliminating its traditional unbalance—is progressively questioned. Furthermore, criteria that confer importance to the attention to the pressing social problems that hinder economic growth, and that deny credibility to a development model that excludes wide sectors of the population and deepens disparity are emerging. Many a time such criteria are born from the very international financial institutions that put into force tough structural adjustments. These criteria were stated in the Summit and were incorporated in the final documents in which, among others, education and public health objectives are registered. However, it is extremely doubtful that measures to solve the regional problems will ever be undertaken, for the Plan of Action is to be subject to the political will of the governments and the ups-and-downs of the continent on U.S. priority list—as it was demonstrated in Punta del Este twenty seven years ago when the loud statements did not materialize at all.

For those who put their hope on entering NAFTA in a rather immediate future, the Summit was a failure because it did not bring that objective any nearer. Before the meeting started, the United States had begun to displace the emphasis from free trade to free investment for which there are both the necessary consensus and conditions. Besides aiding meddling in the internal affairs of Latin-American countries, the short-term impact of free investment is higher than that of free trade.

Beyond the limited objectives of strengthening the inter-American system through more commitment on

94. Rosa López, "Estados Unidos en tres cumbres," *Visión USA*, 3(10) (December 1994). This publication is edited by the CESEU of the University of Havana.

the part of the OAS and the BID, the Summit of the Americas was a costly U.S. public-relations exercise destined to assure the nations of the hemisphere that the negligence of the past had been overcome.[95]

Even though Latin America has not shown strong signs of having the necessary political will to shape up its own agenda on the modernization process, U.S. attempts to control it has encountered considerable obstacles—like the huge regional social problems, and the diverse and coexisting political cultures. Neither can the history of inter-American relations and the difficulties that might occur in issues like migration be ignored.

Moreover, from the point of view of active participation in international affairs based on negotiation and convergence, the politico-ideological climate within the United States is evolving in the wrong direction. Rightism of U.S. politics—which finds echoes in some sectors of the population (above all in the affected middle class)— does not augur well to a foreign projection in which the economic and diplomatic tools effectively replace naked force.

Until the mid-term congressional elections were celebrated in November 1994, the internal political debate had stayed in the center—excluding the extremes. Those elections however displaced the debate to the right. The Republican victory not only meant controlling both Houses of the federal Congress but also that the elected congressmen and senators advocate the new trends within the Republican Party.

As post-war consensus crumbled and the liberal positions that extolled the benefactor state and a strong international presence lost ground—a phenomenon reflecting erosion of U.S. worldwide preeminence—the conservatism that enthroned in U.S. politics since the mid-70s has made gradual advances and permeated all social ambits.

95. Ibid.

Through a populist manipulation of the issues, in the elections the Republican Party has been able to capitalize on the growing feeling of unsatisfaction and frustration within U.S. middle class as a result of governmental policies that are considered elitist and removed from the true concerns of the workers.

Within the party lines there is a segregationist wing that returns to the "internationalist" trend clearly expressed in the 80s by the Reagan and Bush administrations. The new generation of Republicans the federal Congress consists of for the most part is skeptical of foreign aid, suspicious of granting assistance for Russian reforms, and doubtful of the effectiveness of UN performance. Its main national-security initiative—the revival of a strategic defense shield—bears implicit the purpose of building up an "America fortress" in response to the challenges of the international context.

Congress control by the Republican Party has turned into an activation of the legislative branch aimed at robbing a democratic Executive of the initiative and conforming the agenda according to Republican conceptions and interests.

In the House of Representatives such activation became more definite through a political platform called "Contract with America" headed by former Speaker of the House Newt Gingrich, the representative from Georgia. Although the Senate did not adhere to this platform, it has maintained a confrontational attitude before the Executive during the Clinton administration. This attitude has been headed by Senator Robert Dole—leader of the majority and main aspirant to the Republican nomination as president candidate—and Senator Jesse Helms—president of the powerful Foreign Relations Committee.

The legislation on foreign policy introduced by Republican initiative in the 104th session of the Congress is directed to deprive the president of a number of structures and mechanisms. Most of them are beyond congressional control and emerged at a historical moment in which the Executive concentrated and centralized a lot of power to answer the diversity of global-expansion state interests.

The proposal—announced by Senator Helms in March 1995— to eliminate the U.S. Information Agency (USIA), the U.S. Agency for International Development (USAID), and the Arms Control and Disarmament Agency (ACDA) clearly shows the intentions to reduce the Executive prerogatives in conducting foreign policy.

This sophisticated design—which involves restructuring the Department of State for it to absorb part of the functions of the independent agencies to be eliminated, and the creation of the International Foundation for Development—shows the conservative conceptions on key issues like public diplomacy, bilateral aid for foreign development, and arms control. Regarding foreign aid, the purpose is to direct the programs toward attaining U.S. policy specific interests and channel them through international financial institutions, nongovernmental organizations, and private-sector investment.

Although those proposals did not progress during 1995, they have not been abandoned by their promoters. Such conceptions keep on cutting their way into the Congress. The discussion on the Department of State and foreign-aid budgets may be an example. Then the Republican legislative majority proposed dramatic cuts which affect not only the funds allocated to NATO, OAS, and UN peace operations but also those for aiding Africa, Latin America, the Caribbean, and the Asia-Pacific region. Half the allocations however is destined to Egypt, Israel, and other U.S. strategic allies.

These budget cuts will lower U.S. foreign aid (less than 1% of the foreign-policy budget) down to insignificant levels. During the fiscal year 1995, the United

States used 16 million dollars for this concept. It was 21% less than in the 1986 budget.

The financial Mexican crisis—which started just a few days after the Summit of the Americas was held in Miami, and a year after NAFTA was put into force—has had negative repercussions related to U.S. integrating impulse in the hemisphere.

Republicans—the main promoters of those agreements—are now reticent to go on with the process involved. (In this respect, the Initiative for the Caribbean Basin during the Reagan administration, and both NAFTA and the Initiative for the Americas during the Bush Administration must be recalled.) Moreover, the opposition of some groups within the Democratic Party which have objected the agreements based on their concern in the potential labor affectations in various U.S. productive sectors and other environmental issues is to be added to the Republican reticence.

Although the Clinton administration has demonstrated it is politically willing to continue moving toward the objective of creating a free-trade area in the Americas by 2005—as it has been exemplified by the Continental Conference of Trade Ministers, held in Denver, Colorado, in June 1995—it is facing substantial obstacles—like the Congress negative vote to pass on the "fast way" to incorporate Chile to NAFTA—to achieve it.

The Republican control of the national agenda —which the continental integrating measures hang from—, the very ambiguity of the Administration—which debates itself between free-trade support and the application of sanctions and quotas, typical of the "commercial imperialism"—, and the disregard for Latin America in favor of the Asia-Pacific area form an extremely unfavorable picture for North-South relations in this zone of the world where—regardless of the future international order and the place the United States takes within it—U.S. projection is a key factor to define probable scenarios.

The International Scenarios of Cuba-U.S. Conflict

The Permanent Context
—The North-South Relation

The historical pattern of Cuba-U.S. relations is one of the factors to be taken into account on analyzing the bilateral conflict today—while the East-West conditioning has been removed, the conflict still keeps many of the features it gained during the Cold War. Moreover, Cuba is excluded from the design the United States attempts to develop in the hemisphere.

Once the conditions of rigid bipolarity in which the conflict evolved for three decades disappeared, the main feature of this historical pattern emerges: the irreconcilability between the existence of a sovereign state in Cuba and the hegemonical pretensions of the United States that denies a small country close to U.S. shores the right to exercise independence—which is considered both harmful to U.S. essential interests and a threat to its national security.

That geopolitical view of the world has been animating U.S. policy toward Cuba since long before the Island gained its formal independence from Spain. Official statements made, and actions undertaken, by successive U.S. governments for two centuries are a solid body of historical evidence on the fact. It does not only explain the poignancy of the conflict but also the inability to wholly consider it a consequence of the Cold War and, therefore, subject to the conditions that put an end to such form of international order.

This policy of denying Cuba the right to become the sovereign actor of its decisions has had diverse manifestations. To begin with, in the 19th century the United States tried to buy Cuba, and later on it hindered the independence process in the Island until conditions for annexation were ripe. When the success of the Cuban fight for independence was imminent, the United States intervened militarily to avoid the triumph of the nationalist forces, and imposed a U.S. protectorate on the Island. The legacy of such policy continued expressing itself all along the neocolonial republic inaugurated in 1902. Over this period the economic dependency on the United States—which had started during the Spanish colonial dominance—was coupled with the most humiliating political subordination.[96]

Therefore, although it is true that since the 1959 revolutionary triumph—and even after the strategic-military, politico-ideological, and economic alliance with the USSR was concerted—, the Cuba-U.S. conflict was framed within the strategic confrontation between the superpowers. Its permanent context is the North-South problem.

By placing the Cuba-U.S. conflict in the North-South perspective one does not try to reduce the complexity and diversity of mutually excluding interests to the economic contradictions that typify the center-periphery relation. As it has been demonstrated, the North-South problem is much more diverse and far-ranging. And although it has an economic basis, it is not in fact a con-

96. For a compilation of U.S. statements and actions regarding Cuba during the 19th and the 20th centuries, refer to *Agresiones de Estados Unidos a Cuba 1787-1976* (La Habana: Editorial de Ciencias Sociales, 1979).

frontation between different cultural proposals. So, for the South countries, independence is translated into the possibility of preserving their identities, and sovereignty means the assurance of being able to do with their natural and human resources to face the assault from the North, which pretends to make the rest of the planet serve its survival.

However it is not a matter of finding another axis of fundamental contradictions that replaces the East-West confrontation and considering the North-South problem as a new asymmetric bipolarism, for it would not only reduce international relations to a confrontational scheme between the rich and the poor but also would disregard the specific weight of angles like intra-North competition, the countless sources of conflict plaguing the South, and the existence of a number of global problems.

Inasmuch as the confrontational scenario of the late 1990s does not seem to be moving into an eventual solution—despite the deep transformations occurred not only in both societies but also in the international context—, our purpose is to place the phenomenon of continuous U.S. hostility toward Cuba, and Cuban determination to maintain a national independence project in their right perspective.

Consequently, to reach a better understanding of the Cuba-U.S. conflict—whether in its historical evolvement or in its present state—, it is necessary to approach it from two angles: (1) the North-South problem in its wider sense—which considers its origin and continuity—, and (2) its features relative to its position in the East-West confrontation—which has not been lost in spite of the fact the Cold War is over.

In view of the strategic bipolarity between the superpowers, there was a tendency to relegate the North-South angle when pondering over the conflict; notwithstanding it was ever present. It must be noticed the subordinate role such contradictions played in an international system dominated by the essential contradiction between two antagonistic socioeconomic systems: capitalism and socialism.

The very revolutionary process in Cuba—which tries to answer the long-time frustrated aspirations to achieve political independence and a social-justice regime, i.e., entirely belonging to the problem conceptualized in the North-South conflict—has met U.S. hostility since its beginning. As to United States' standpoint, such kind of project meant a fissure in its hemispheric hegemony system, and so it is as unacceptable as the reformist design headed by President Jacobo Arbenz in Guatemala few years before.

Following the highly ideological view of the world that any progress of the revolutionary forces in the political field meant a loss for the United States and a net profit for its strategic rival, all popular movements in the so-called Third World were automatically met with a hostile answer from U.S. policy. Such an advance happening in the Western Hemisphere, in the Caribbean, and in Cuba—an area under U.S. control and from where the United States projects its international hegemony and leadership—motivated a vicious reaction that deepened the interest conflict between the two states, and originated a dynamic of permanent confrontation.

This dynamic of permanent confrontation conjugated the fact that the Island belonged to the pole led by the USSR, and the identification of other scenarios—the Third World in general, and Latin America in particular—where Cuba tried to promote its own interests.[97]

Thus, many of the policies developed by Cuba and a great number of its international actions—directed to both strengthening its position in response to U.S. hos-

97. Carlos Rafael Rodríguez, "Fundamentos estratégicos de la Revolución Cubana," in *Letra con filo*, vol.1 (La Habana: Editorial de Ciencias Sociales, 1983), 376.

tility, and guaranteeing its security—were either simply considered to be part of the Soviet—or "communist"—design to dispute U.S. hegemony in some regions of the planet, or bombed by the rhetorical arsenal of "refraining" to render them illegal. Of course, it does not deny that international dynamic—set by the confrontation between two powers whose economic, political and social regimes were antagonistic—granted rationality to such a perception that disregarded individual considerations about Cuban action in the international arena.

The policy of the United States toward Cuba—designed to revert the Island's detachment from U.S. orbit—has sparelessly used the foreign-policy guiding tools a great power may avail itself of—most often than not from naked force positions, quite rarely recurring to the negotiation element. In addition to having enjoyed ample consensus in the Democratic and the Republican parties, this policy has been very coherent and consistent despite minor adjustments and approach changes resulting from the transformations occurred in the international context and in the relative position of both countries within it.

This coherence and consistency of the U.S. policy toward Cuba responds to the strategic nature of its goals. These have remained unaltered over the years. Its three basic pillars are economic blockade, absence of diplomatic recognition, and international isolation. And within this matrix of economic, political, and diplomatic pressures, the main direction of U.S. aggressions has moved.

However, the Cuban decision to adopt socialism as a socioeconomic system responded not only to the realization by the revolutionary leadership that a national independence project could not be developed within the capitalist ambit at the gates of the biggest superpower ever, but also to the need to protect the revolutionary process from U.S. aggressiveness through gaining Soviet Union support.

Neither the ideological inclination nor the security imperatives that urged Cuba to follow the socialist way to development made it deny that it objectively belonged to the problems affecting underdeveloped countries. What is more, Cuban international projection has always bestowed great relevance upon the Third World dimension in general and the Latin American one in particular. These are additional guarantors of its security before U.S. hostility and the limitations of its alliance with the Soviet Union—the latter shown during the October Crisis. Both dimensions became serious tension sources with the Unites States and issues of the bilateral conflict.

While the "disconnection" of Cuba from the world capitalist system—where it had a place in the periphery-South as exporter of raw materials, importer of merchandise and capital, and investment receptor—enabled it to reach a certain degree of development that was translated into the improvement of social conditions, Cuba could neither gain economic independence nor overcome underdevelopment, i.e., the structural deformities of economy. Although the insertion of Cuba in the socialist-camp market was advantageous in terms of prices, credits and supplies, it did not mean Cuban economy diversification or dramatic achievements on the way to industrialization.

The disappearance of the European socialism and the U.S.S.R. as a multinational state made Cuba plunge into the worst economic crisis of its history at the beginning of the 1990s. The rupture of its relations meant much more than losing some 80% of its commercial bonds. Cuba lost not only privileged economic links with a community of nations but also its only steady source of foreign credit and financing. In short, Cuba abruptly lost the ambit in which its economy had been tightly and deeply integrated.

So, the impact of the disappearance of the international bipolarism that had acted as context when the Cuban revolution triumphed—context in which the alliance with the U.S.S.R. and the socialist camp had been one of the elements guaranteeing Cuban national security—manifested in both domestic and international affairs.

However, the disappearance of the socialist camp and the Soviet Union had tougher repercussions within the Cuban society. The disarticulation of the international economic relation system Cuba had been participating in for three decades—and whose involvement was almost 85% of its foreign economic activity—occurred at a time the Cuban economy had not been as yet able to overcome its highly dependent and hardly diversified nature, or the inefficiency of its production system. The high-priority attention bestowed upon economic development in the 1970s had not been backed up by a consistent economic practice.

Due to the mid-1970s consolidation of the politico-ideological alliance between Cuba and the U.S.S.R., their economic relations were subordinated to political decision which most of the time ignored the principles that should govern commercial, credit, and financial operations. The situation became complex and contradictory.

While the principles guiding the economic Cuba-U.S.S.R. and Cuba-CMEA relations were based on fair considerations for they were a way of helping the development of a small and poor country (one of the greatest problems faced by humanity without a solution even in the post-Cold War era), diverse kind of factors made the inefficiency aspects associated to the socialist practice in Europe and disguised by the relevance of the political decisions to be transferred to our economy together with the assistance.

The question whether it was right or not for Cuba —under the imperative of guaranteeing its national security in a surrounding world particularly hostile to the Revolution—to assume the harms—derived from an integration whose capacity to become an economic-independence factor was limited—together with the obvious benefits, lies open.

It cannot be forgotten that the U.S. policy of economic blockade to Cuba enforced in 1962 prevented the Island from choosing which type of economic relations were to be developed. Thus U.S. policy became an element that conditioned the area of international trade in which Cuba might insert itself—provided it were an open economy. The other obstacle to achieve acceptable levels of economic efficiency is related to the impossibility for the Cuban economic management to make the development strategies match the implementation practice.

As a consequence of the debacle experimented by socialism at international scale, there started a period in Cuba in which it was imperative for it to reach an economic dynamic of its own, and to improve its political system—cardinal issues to guarantee its security as an independent state. As never before it became absolutely necessary to conjugate the foreign policy and the domestic one harmoniously.

In an international context in which the politico-ideological alliances have all but vanished and the economic factor is prone to decide the role and place of every country in the concert of nations, it must be a goal of the Cuban foreign policy to help reach its own economy dynamic to maximize the Island's security.

However, although it is once again stated that the Cold War is over—a historic period during which Cuba had to give top priority to military defense—, U.S. policy toward the Island provoked that the military and the economic components of Cuban security were kept at the priority level they were during the East-West confrontation.

Since the disappearance of the USSR, Cuba—disconnected from the prevailing economic practices—had to assume its condition of underdeveloped country and to search for its reinsertion in a quite different international context. The force correlation had changed dramatically over the last few decades of the 20th century. The matters that had seemed to be substantial achievements of noncapitalist production relations—which allowed alternative models to be developed—not only flopped but reversed. It resulted in the propagation of the economic, political, and ideological view of the capitalist central countries, and the reduction of the number of available options to those governments that like the Cuban one persisted in developing a national project outside —though not isolated from—the increasingly globalized capitalist system.

An international context undergoing a transition and a U.S. foreign policy tightening its hostility toward Cuba are the cores in which the Cuban foreign policy reorientation takes place. Although the transition into globalization is an objective phenomenon, it must be accepted it is being conducted by "the Centers" according to their politico-economic interests and from increasingly coordinated positions. As it has been previously stated, the South is assigned a segregated role. Therefore, the Cuba-U.S. conflict will have to insert itself into a dynamic specially disadvantageous for Cuba.

The North-South relations gained renewed relevance for Cuba as this problem (1) raises its profile within international relations with the disappearance of the Second World and the irrelevancy of talking about a Third World; (2) acquires a new dynamic as a result of the globalization process; (3) is one of the main contexts in which Cuban foreign policy will evolve since this is the framework for its reinsertion in a world economy, and the need to associate to foreign capital; and (4) is the context in which the conflict with the United States will evolve. Regardless of the relative loss of preeminence in the international system, the United States still is a first-degree power in the world. It strongly projects its hegemony in the geographic area where Cuba is located. There it should broaden and strengthen its politico-economic relations as a result of common language and traditions, cultural affinities, and development degree.

There precisely lies the complex peculiarity of the Cuba-U.S. conflict in its present form. In its broader sense, Cuba—inasmuch as a South country since the origins of capitalist internationalization—is part of the North-South contradictions in the process of transition into globalization. Consequently, the predictable trends for the countries in the unfavored pole—discussed in the second chapter—are the global scenario for the immediate development of Cuba.

For instance, one of the challenges the economic globalization poses to Cuba consists of its need to simultaneously embark on the recovery and further development of the economy, and on a radical transformation of its insertion into world economy. But to achieve this, Cuba must satisfy a set of conditions—for example, the development of new productions or the modification of the existing ones to the point of reaching competitive levels similar to or even higher than the ones in the world market. Attaining such a goal demands promoting actions, introducing completely new criteria on costs, labor productivity, prices, efficiency and management, and incorporating technical and scientific breakthroughs into the production processes.

The technical and scientific development means other multiphase challenge for Cuba. Considering the relevance gained by the technical and scientific factor in the present conditions—and those in the future—, Cuba must reinsert itself in a world economy in which competitiveness is rapidly changing as a result of inventions and breakthroughs.

The huge expenses demanded by the R&D branch, and the risks and uncertainties associated with it make it unthinkable that an underdeveloped nation could invest in all fields and, least of all, compete with the great world powers and their transnational companies. So, Cuba must make a profound analysis of the leading sectors or products showing optimal conditions for international competition and find its niche in world economy.

The technical and scientific challenge has other dimensions for Cuban economy. On the one hand, the competitiveness search involves the introduction of state-of-the-art technologies, and these for the most part are labor-saving. This feature results contradictory with the current employment situation in the country. On the other hand, the transformations to be effected on Cuban economy are already forcing the authorities to take measures to undertake a widespread labor requalification program in the near future. Such a program would enable the work force to assimilate the new technologies and/or to solve the prevailing demand-supply disequilibrium of qualifications in the country.

Moreover, Cuba will apparently have to continue defying the U.S. blockade which does not seem prone to a short-term relaxation due to the influence of very conservative sectors within the U.S. government. Its more recent expression is the Helms-Burton Law oriented toward tightening and internationalizing the blockade.

In this respect, a study carried out by the Instituto de Relaciones Europeo-Latinoamericanas (IRELA) (Institute for European-Latin American Relations) based in Madrid contended: "Probably the most powerful limitation to Cuban politics and the obstacle posing the most adverse effects to the regime's economic program is the U.S.

embargo—and even more so are the policies and the support from the Cuban exiled community that have perpetuated it."[98]

But just as the globalization process is not free from contradictions among the blocs—contradictions that are increasingly tougher—, among the bloc-leading powers, and among the bloc-member nations, the situation of the international context becomes uncertain and changing. This situation not only poses a challenge to Cuba, but also is a space to maximize its national independence, sovereignty, and self-determination goals by capitalizing on the profit margins such contradictions might generate.

This complex bunch of circumstances conditions the evolvement of the Cuba-U.S. conflict. While Cuba is geographically located within the U.S. sphere of influence —a historical phenomenon transcending the immediate Cold War past—it shows the discrepancies between the hemispheric poles. The disregard of the United States for the grave economic and social conditions prevailing in Latin America and the state of undisputed hegemony it enjoys generate tensions whose consequences Cuba cannot escape from.

The huge challenge of achieving—from underdevelopment—a successful reinsertion in a globalized economy opened to new forms of competition is added to the tightening of U.S. hostility. The United States considers the current international conditions as a validation of the political, philosophical, and religious principles and ideas supporting the U.S. society's self-assigned notion of messianism as a consequence of its performance and world leadership.

Additionally the worsening of the Cuba-U.S. conflict during the Cold War has left imprints that explain the

98. IRELA, *Cuba en crisis: Procesos y perspectivas* (Madrid, 1994), 25.

reason for a Washington-imposed Cuban policy. Today it keeps the features it had during the bipolar confrontation and only tangentially assumes some of the issues belonging to the new North-South agenda—environmental protection, narcotraffic, democracy, human rights. These are made to serve hostility rather than political and diplomatic influence.

Besides, the essential subjects of the above-mentioned agenda—free trade and capital investment—are completely excluded from the current policy of the United States relative to Cuba . It can just be defined as an obvious example of the renewed strength gained by the "old thought" within U.S. power structures as far as Cuba is concerned.

The economic pressures and aggressions aimed at strangling and delegitimizing prevail over the attitude that has been perfectly outlined—toward other areas, countries, and regions—in the reconstruction process of the definition of U.S. national interest; i.e., the need to spread over and deepen up capitalist production forms in the underdeveloped South to strengthen U.S. economy.

Cuban Foreign-Policy Adjustment

At a moment of growing conviction that the course of the objective process of globalization is forcing the United States to pay attention to the relegated South end of the hemisphere and to implement new policies directed to an increased integration with South economies—through an adequate society homogenization with U.S.-promoted values—, the United States maintains its policy of economic blockade, absence of normal diplomatic relations, and international isolation toward Cuba. Therefore, Cuba has to rearrange its international economical and political relations in a world in which it is attempted

to universalize a neoliberal model conceived as a consolidation of the trends the centers want to impose on
global capitalism. Such consolidation stipulates not only
economic homogenization of the countries from the
adoption of its capitalist principles and institutions
—free international trade, currency convertibility, privat-
ization as the main growth drive, corporative property as
the principal form of organizing big companies, openness to foreign investment, and membership in key international economic organizations (IMF, WB, and
WTO)[99]—but also incorporating a number of values of
the western political culture embodied in bourgeois democracy.

To carry out such a rearrangement, Cuba has had to
adjust the principles of its foreign policy. The Fourth
Congress of the Communist Party of Cuba (CPC), held
in October 1991, showed, among its outcomes, the
elaboration of a new Resolution on Foreign Policy, and
the recommendation to introduce modifications to the
1976 Constitution of the Republic of Cuba. Both in the
above-mentioned documents and in others voted on by
the assembly, the existence of a new international context is acknowledged. It recommends changes in the
domestic and international political practice of Cuba.
Consequently, reforms on the Constitution of the Republic were passed.

The new identifying signs of the current international
situation and the necessary adjustments to the principles and objectives of Cuban foreign policy were incorporated to the modifications to the Constitutional Law
—legalized by the Asamblea Nacional del Poder Popular
in October 1992—and to the above-mentioned Resolution on Foreign Policy of the Fourth Congress of the CPC.

In the Resolution on Foreign Policy it is stated that the
most relevant international events are the disappear-

99. Jeffrey D. Sach, "Consolidating Capitalism," in *Foreign Policy* 98
(Spring 1995), 51.

ance of socialism in East Europe, and the progressive weakening and growing danger of extinction of the USSR (it became a fact only two months later). Because of this, the international situation is described as the scenario of the "biggest global realignment of economic, political, and military forces since the end of World War II, and it doubtlessly involves the toughest blow for the communists, the revolutionaries, and all the peoples on Earth in the present century."[100]

There is also noticed that the war on the Persian Gulf—which had been capitalized on by the United States to show off its military power and technological supremacy—has consolidated U.S. unipolarity. However, in the economic competition the United States is in no condition to "occupy . . . the same hegemonic place it has . . . in the military field."[101]

Finally there is stated that the growing tendency to form economic blocs—the United States, the Economic Community and Japan—"progressively segregates the underdeveloped countries, which demands their unity and economic integration as an imperative need."[102]

Increasing poverty in Third World countries—despite the use of neoliberal mechanisms—shows the lack of capacity of capitalism to solve the most pressing problems of over four billion people in the world. Poor living conditions are culture broth for potential social upheavals.

U.S. post-Cold War policy toward Cuba was not changed upon U.S. perception that the international context—on the disappearance of the USSR and the East European socialism—was so unfavorable for the Island that the means employed at the time were more effective than in the past and so the objectives were to be attained without assuming the expenses any policy change involves.

100. "Resolución sobre política exterior," in *IV Congreso del PCC, discursos y documentos* (La Habana: Editora Política, 1992), 350.
101. Ibid., 352.
102. Ibid.

Since it was no longer possible to make reference to either the international play of the Island or the Cuban-Soviet connection to justify hostility, the focus was changed and the emphasis was placed on the internal situation of Cuba and on aspects of its political system. Then the essence of the conflict stood naked: hegemony-sovereignty.

Although such an orientation of U.S. policy toward Cuban internal affairs has always been present, now it is incorporated in both post-Cold War conditions and the patterns that the United States—and North countries in general—tries to force upon South countries, i.e., market economy and liberal democracy. However, these tools based on such a design are not favored, and those defined during the Cold War are maintained and tightened.

U.S. policy toward Cuba—since 1992 embodied in the system of tools known as the Torricelli Law—supposedly belongs to the canons established to spread democracy according to the already mentioned model. The Torricelli Law consists of two tracks which either allow to employ pressure elements—like the economic blockade—or to implement measures for value transmission through "people-to-people" approach to a "pacific subvertion"—like communications improvements, cultural exchanges, etcetera.

In truth, so far only one of the tracks has operated—the hostility track. It means that the policy designed during the Cold War still stands, and the paths that might lead to a gradual approach progressively close. What in theory was a "cudgel and carrot" cocktail, in practice it is sheer cudgel. The purpose of denying legitimacy to the Cuban project and the thirst to punish its present direction overcome the intentions to aid a transition in the Cuban society according to U.S. strategic goals in a region where the U.S. economic-pressure policy toward Cuba is mostly rejected as it has been shown in diverse international forums—the United Nations among them.

In such a global context that aids tightening U.S. hostility toward Cuba, the leadership of the Island has defined the principles and scenarios of a foreign policy oriented to rearrange the bases to guarantee its national security.

LATIN AMERICA AND THE CARIBBEAN

The 1976 Cuban constitutional text and the Theses and Resolution on Foreign Policy of the First Congress of the CPC considered the relations with the USSR and the rest of the socialist camp strategic while Cuban-Latin American relations were second-ranked. In the documents that have been regulating Cuban foreign policy since 1991, Latin America and the Caribbean have returned to the high-priority place they had along the 1960s. However, principles like *Latin-Americanism* and *anti-imperialism* have been duly adequated to the current international reality.

The constitutional reforms echoed the modifications that were taking place worldwide in the field of anti-imperialist fight. In keeping with this, the imperialist and neocolonialist policy—which pursues limiting and subordinating the sovereignty of Latin American peoples while deepens the conditions of exploitation and oppression of underdeveloped nations—is utterly condemned, and there is a general call for unity among the so-called Third World countries.[103]

In the Preamble to the Cuban Constitution it is stated that the decision to build the Communist society is based on "proletarian internationalism, fraternal friendship, aid, cooperation, and solidarity among the peoples of Latin America, the Caribbean rim and the rest of the world."[104]

103. Ibid., 355.
104. Asamblea Nacional del Poder Popular, *Proyecto de modificaciones a la Constitución de la República*, (La Habana), 2.

The functioning of the Cuban relations with Latin America and the Caribbean—as a support to the development of the Cuban national project—is based on considering their state. In this respect, the relevance of the First Iberian American Summit is highlighted as it "was a significant step on the road to integrating the peoples of our continent. Its celebration without U.S. presence clearly showed our common identity , and the will to advance together toward the necessary integration as to achieve the real independence that allows us to reach the place we deserve in today's world and the world of the future."[105]

Although it is acknowledged there are difficulties to attain the above-mentioned purposes, the roles of language, historic traditions, and common problems are considered to be "favorable conditions for such necessary unity."

In order to attain the integration and collaboration with Latin-American and Caribbean countries[106]—without the specifications contained in article 12 of the 1976 Constitution about the integration with Latin-American countries after the liberation from foreign dominance and internal oppressions in the common fight against colonialism, neocolonialism, and imperialism—, a joint policy to face the situations that burden our countries is incorporated as a goal. In this sense, it is necessary to "begin—as it has been done lately—by regional and subregional agreements that may be turned into wider ways to Latin American integration. The experiences so far accumulated—and even the unexploited potentialities—reveal the existing possibilities and stress the need for integration."[107]

105. "Resolución," op. cit., 354.
106. Ibid.
107. Ibid.

Nowadays the readjustment of the Cuban economic model is—as never before—the main basis to guarantee national security. Cuban foreign policy is to see to this requirement. Therefore, the position stated by President Fidel Castro in Guadalajara on offering Latin American investors preference conditions to propitiate the process is reiterated.[108]

In favor of Latin-American economic integration and political coordination, Cuban foreign policy grants special relevance to such summits, that is, to the scenario for the debate on the problems of the region without U.S. presence. Likewise, although Cuba is against accepting the exclusive right of a few countries to own nuclear weapons, it stated its disposition to sign the Treaty of Tlatelolco to favor Latin-American unity.[109]

The progress of Cuban-Latin American relations in the 1970s and the 1980s became the basis for reorienting Cuban foreign policy after USSR disappearance and, consequently, one of the guaranteeing elements of Cuban security within a changing—although unipolar—system of international relations. In such a system the survival of the Cuban revolutionary project has the reinsertion in the international market among its most important challenges.

Cuban economic insertion in Latin America and the Caribbean must overcome two considerable obstacles: the lack of complementarity—in a traditional sense—of the regional economies and the growing process of transnationalization of Latin-American economy. The NAFTA talks in favor of the strengthening of neoliberal control mechanisms over the region. There must be added that the fabricated mirage that belonging to a given bloc protects nations from segregation, is causing most Latin-American countries focus their hopes on

108. Ibid., 356.
109. Ibid., 355.

such kind of association and are ready to allow a lot of concessions.

Despite the fact that, in Latin America and the Caribbean, voted-in governments via democratic elections predominate, the deterioration of the living conditions following the application of the neoliberal economic model is translated into the political unrest prevailing in most countries.

The replacement of military dictatorships with duly elected governments has kept unchanged the problems related to a way of power exercise that reproduces the conditions of extreme political, economic, and social weakness.

Facing such a situation, the weakness of Latin-American societies means considerable obstacles for Cuban foreign policy based on integration and cooperation with Latin America. The United States capitalizes on such weakness in its policy against Cuba .

To revert such a situation, Cuba counts on its potentiality to develop state-of-the-art technologies, and its high capacity to solve Third World technologic and service problems—taking into account that technical solutions generally come from highly developed countries whose climate and production conditions differ from the ones in underdeveloped countries. It generates new fields that make integration and cooperation feasible.

The shortage of investment resources plaguing the Latin-American economic arena finds a way to improvement in Cuban preference for Latin-American capital. The same is true for the diverse forms of production and marketing cooperation Cuba has favored, for joint ventures between the domestic and Latin-American capital not necessarily involve high investment volumes. It is due to the fact that Cuban economy has two significant factors: a highly-qualified labor force, and important industrial facilities that only need modernization and market for their productions.

In the politico-diplomatic domain, there is room for its development. For most Latin American countries the relation with Cuba is a national-sovereignty element which attempts to compensate the subordination to the United States.

Finally, the demonstration of the authentic character of the Cuban economic, political, and social project becomes a key factor to the progress of the objectives of Cuba's Latin-American policy.

The Resolution on Foreign Policy also ratified and maintained as constitutional concept, the principle of *pacific coexistence*. It also involves the goal of Cuban foreign policy toward the United States on the economic blockade, the return of the territory occupied by the naval base in Guantánamo, and the willingness to solve the conflict issues based on mutual respect for sovereignty, independence, and equality.[110]

RUSSIA AND EAST-EUROPEAN COUNTRIES

Regarding the new countries in the former USSR and the ones that had renounced to socialism in East Europe, the Cuban foreign-policy objective—based on the consideration that those countries had had friendly relations with Cuba for three decades—is directed to foster bilateral relations "in the prevailing conditions based on the ever-present mutual respect, continuity of the relations in all possible fields and ways."[111]

Political and military unsteadiness and economic anarchy have so far prevented the implementation of mutually profitable relations between Cuba and the independent republics of the former U.S.S.R.

The market of the new Eurasian countries is still significant for Cuba—even while undergoing a reorientation of their foreign trade. In the short and medium

110. Ibid., 351.
111. Ibid., 359-60.

term, this is the market where important volumes of sugar, nickel, citric fruits, and medical and biotechnological products should be placed, and the market to buy spare parts, fuel, armaments, and food from.

Therefore, regarding the relations with the new Eurasian countries, Cuba emphasizes its willingness to maintain bonds with them—especially economic mutually-profitable relations. However, considering the volume of commercial exchange and type of production, Russia is the most important among them.

U.S. pressures should be taken into account in case there might be any reanimation of Cuban economy. So as soon as a restructuration of Cuba-Russia economic relation is detected, the canceling mechanism will be activated.

INDUSTRIALIZED COUNTRIES

The CPC Congress in 1991 also considered "a right policy . . . that has procured relations with Third World countries and has also been opened to trade and collaboration with industrialized capitalist countries. Consequently, it is considered necessary to expand and deepen—on mutually profitable basis—the relations of our country with the European Community, all the nations of this continent, and also Canada and Japan."[112]

The Cuban moratorium of its foreign debt with countries of the European Community, Canada and Japan continues to be a limitation to expand the commercial and financial links between Cuba and those countries. However, new forms of economic relations are opening up mainly related to boosting investments in sectors like tourism and other industrial branches.

The speed of the investment flow from those countries will directly depend on the efficiency gained by Cu-

112. Ibid., 356.

ban economy, the contractual guarantees on business, and the perception of stability in Cuban society.

The competition of the new Eurasian countries in the international investment market and the interest of European capitals in getting a place in their own geographical region will jeopardize the flow toward the Third World in general, and toward Cuba in particular.

It must be noticed that all those U.S.-allied countries have unanimously rejected the extra-territorial nature of enforcing clauses regarding the trade between Cuba and the rest of the world contained in the Torricelli Law. However, it does not mean that U.S. pressures to prevent Cuban reinsertion in the international commerce are not successful. Although the present economic reforms in Cuba are directed to assure the insertion in the world economy, they have not followed the pattern promoted by the United States. While the Cuban relations with the rest of the North countries are not free from conditionings, they are established with due respect for state sovereignty and based on mutual benefit.

Despite the attempts of some members of the Movement of Non-Aligned Countries to eliminate it under the assumption that only economic fight would determine the course of international events once the Cold War ended, Cuba maintains *nonalignment* as one of the main principles of its foreign policy. Although one of the military blocs has disappeared, "the imperialist and neocolonialist policy that limits and subordinates the sovereignty of our countries survives. At the same time, the economic conditions of exploitation and oppression of underdeveloped nations are getting worse instead of finding a solution."[113]

Therefore, the Cuban non-alignment policy pursues "the unification of the peoples of the so-called Third World," this being one of the new concepts on foreign policy adopted by the Cuban Constitution.

113. Asamblea Nacional del Poder Popular, op. cit., 11.

Cuba proclaims its capacity to aid a negotiated solution of the conflicts—like it did in the case of southwestern Africa—as testimony of its policy toward the Third World. Objectives like the struggle of the Third World in the United Nations to solve global problems—for instance, the new world economic order, peaceful solution for regional conflicts, peace strenghtening, and democratization of the UN Security Council—were included again in the documents ruling Cuban foreign policy since 1991.[114] Hence, Cuban persistence on strengthening the Movement of Nonaligned Countries and its representative levels.

The 9th Summit of this Movement—the most important international entity of Third World countries—held in Belgrade, Yugoslavia, faced a weakening period which was justly considered as the beginning of its disappearance. The celebration of the 10th Summit in Jakarta, Indonesia, in September 1992, was the occasion for Cuban nonalignment objectives to become a reality. Among the goals of the Cuban delegation were:

1. The attendance of 102 out of the 108 member countries to a meeting in which it would be decided whether the Movement was to continue or not.
2. The considerations that—in a unipolar world— the Movement's original purposes are yet to be accomplished. So, a common place was found to coordinate actions within the United Nations against the structuring of a new world order that excludes Third World countries.
3. The active participation of the Cuban delegation collaborated to gather its points of view regarding human rights, extraterritoriality of the powers, terrorism tolerance, coordination of actions directed to reforming the United Nations system, etcetera in the documents passed.

114. "Resolución," 357.

4. The trust that Indonesia was presiding the Movement favoring its promotion, consolidation, and development. Cuba acknowledges Indonesia has a position close to the freedom of criteria expressed by countries like Egypt, Malaysia, and those in Southeast Asia, which are opposed to establish universally homogeneous cultural patterns.

5. The identification of potentialities to foster commercial exchange and cooperation in the South.

6. The creation of a Ministerial Committee for Economic Development.

Ricardo Alarcón, Cuban chancellor at the time, stated that, regardless of the existing distance between word and action on a unanimous consensus, a common and open language about the dangers of unipolarity and the new world order was gained in Jakarta. The latter issue affects all member countries alike and will be the basis for potential coordinated actions in the international arena.[115]

The 1996 Summit of the Movement in Cartagena de Indias, Colombia, is a milestone for it and might even be conclusive for its future. For the second time in the history of this Movement, a Latin-American country is elected to preside it—Cuba had presided from 1973 to 1976. The presidency pretends to give the organization a non-United States-contesting and more pragmatic orientation. Should this purpose be consolidated, we would face a change of course in favor of the triumph of the positions that consider this Movement useless given the current international conditions—as it has been expressed since the Yugoslavian Summit. That being the case, the advances attained in Jakarta would remain simple declarative exercises.

115. Dr. Baró's notes on "La Cumbre del NOAL ante la nueva situación internacional." The event was held at the Asociación Cubana de Naciones Unidas (ACNU), Havana, September 17, 1992.

An Unsolvable Conflict?

More than five years after the Cold War ended, the Cuba-U.S. conflict has not experienced substantial changes indicating its potential relaxation in the short or medium terms. Cuba therefore keeps on being the target of increased U.S. hostility, while it is excluded from the design the United States plans to implant in the hemisphere.

In the Cuban case, it seems the United States would rather call off such objectives indefinitively than start negotiations—except on the most pressing issues that concern its national security, like emigration.[116] But even under so difficult circumstances like the uncontrolled Cuban exodus during the summer of 1994 that led to an arrangement between both parties, U.S. Administration considered necessary to put into force measures to tighten the blockade. These measures harmed the expressed objective of the Torricelli Law—to increase contacts between both societies.

Far from helping approach, the current policy eludes the possibility of creating a climate of understanding through the implementation of mutual-trust generating actions aimed at laying the foundations for dismantling long years of confrontation and tensions. Such a policy strengthens the conditions that perpetuate the bilateral conflict while affecting the multilateral arena.

Since 1995 however U.S. policy toward Cuba seems to be at a cul-de-sac since the tactical consensus it had enjoyed all along these years has given crumbling signals at governmental levels. On the one hand, the Republican victory in the mid-term elections in November 1994 gave a turn to the debate on Cuba. As a consequence of the advances made by the ultra-right in the

116. Refer to Graciela Chailloux, "La fuerza de los intereses comunes en las relaciones cubano-norteamericanas," *Cuban Review*, 1 (November 1994).

Federal Congress, there was more room for increased-hostility proposals. On the other hand, forces opposed to the use of such a tool of force tried to activate their participation in the discussion on the future course of the policy toward Cuba.[117]

Such breakage of the consensus on the tools to use in order to reach the strategic objectives of U.S. policy toward Cuba developed in a debate of unprecedented intensity which involved academicians, mass media, and businessmen since mid-1992.[118] Somehow the debate is still going on.

Likewise, the recovery signals of the Cuban economy, together with the strength shown by the political leadership of the Island on conducting the reform process, have made the political circles realize the Cuban transition process would neither follow U.S. purposes nor pay the toll due to a change of policy. It has increased the number of participants in a highly polarized debate in which there are factions prone to decreasing tension and aggressiveness levels at one end, and factions demanding maximum aggressiveness at the other.

The Clinton administration tried to maintain the consensus on the Torricelli Law—while the ultra-right fostered the congressional approval of the Helms-Burton Bill,[119] and an activation of the forces in favor of lifting the blockade was observed. These forces involved representatives from the business sector that consider Cuba an emerging market which is being captured by competing capitals.

117. Refer to Soraya Castro Mariño et al., "La política norteamericana hacia Cuba en 1995," CESEU-UH, Havana, November 1995. Typescript.
118. Refer to Rosa López Oceguera, "Cuba en el debate político norteamericano: ¿hacia un nuevo consenso?" *Visión USA* (January 1994).
119. The Bill for Freedom and Democratic Solidarity with Cuba was introduced by Republican Senator Jesse Helms of North Carolina (s. 381) and the Republican Congressman Dan Burton of Indiana (H R 927) to the Senate and the House of Representatives, respectively, in February 1995.

The debate on Cuba transcends the subject matter, which is functionally and symbolically relevant to the discussion on U.S. projections to other highly important issues and questions about which there is not a defined attitude yet. Among these, the kind of relations that should prevail in the hemisphere, the kind of relations when dealing with allies, the tools that should be used on enforcing policies, the new relation between the Executive and the Congress after the Cold War ended, etcetera.

Thus, Cuba becomes a "trial case"[120] which the diverse and antagonistic forces load up with their particular ideological points of view before joining the debate with alternative proposals. But the history of Cuba-U.S. relations does not augur relaxation to the conflict in the short or medium terms even though the U.S. foreign policy decided to follow a less hostile road. Such a decision would only inaugurate a long, complex, and contradictory process whose outcome might attempt to achieve —through other means—the objectives that have been defined for Cuba in U.S. policy for many years now. But, for that to happen, the perception of the U.S. political circles that decide on the policy toward the Island would have to be completely opposed to the one that is conforming the U.S. policy toward Cuba nowadays.

In the meantime, Cuba may take advantage of the new spaces and contradictions of the capitalist system, and so profit from the renewed intra-North competition to secure markets and investment opportunities. Thus, Cuba might diversify its economic partners, and not only reduce the effects of the present U.S. hostility but also the attempts to be absorbed by the United States in the future.

120. Rosa López Oceguera, "Implicaciones políticas del Proyecto de Ley Helms-Burton," *Visión USA* 5(4) (May 1995).

In its projection toward the South and in view of the widespread nature of the crisis the region is going through, Cuba needs to expand, to deepen, and to consolidate its relations in Latin America and the Caribbean, and to explore all possibilities for South-South cooperation. Latin America and the Caribbean show their vulnerability to the current global problems that place them in an unfavorable situation compared to other areas of the planet, like Southeast Asia. It points out to the segregation of Latin America and the Caribbean rather than to overcoming their underdevelopment.

However, Cuban participation in integration spaces, like the Asociación de Estados del Caribe (Caribbean States Association), opens the chances of an ineludible presence in the regional trade. It is so due to the fact that the Group of Three—Venezuela, Colombia, and Mexico—belongs to that organization. Cuba should play a linking role among the diverse integrating processes in progress at both the North end and the South end of the continent.

Many and many-varied are the challenges Cuba faces at the gates of the third millennium, but none is greater than transforming its integration in the world capitalist market into a means to achieve real modernity. It would grant Cuba its own independent dynamic enabling its participation in the international economic relations for the first time in its history of nation-state.

Only if it happens, the idea that the Cuban revolutionary project has come to an end—an idea that has been feeding the shaping process of U.S. policy toward Cuba since the fall of the Berlin Wall—would have lost its validating character. Such being the case, it would not matter whether the Administration is Democratic or Republican—the track one of the Torricelli Law, or the Helms-Burton Law will no longer be considered valid to succeed in returning Cuba to U.S. influence sphere. The dismembering of the to-the-death hostility policy will be unavoidable, and it will give way to serving politico-ideological tools.

Where will the encouragement to start a tactic change in U.S. policy toward Cuba come from? A conclusive answer is not relevant just now. To know the answer it is required a detailed follow-up of the behavior of the diverse factors involved in the shaping of the U.S. policy toward Cuba. However, the course of the events related to Cuba-U.S. relations from 1959 now indicates—as never before—that the reversion factor of the hostility policy is the Cuban reality. Should Cuba demonstrate the feasibility of an independent national project adjusted to the requirements of the modifications occurring in the international relation system, the United States will not be able to delay the application of political tools allowing the existence of a contradictory but distended modus vivendi.

But even under such a circumstance —after the Law for Freedom and Democratic Solidarity with Cuba was passed—the obstacles to be overcome by a change of tactic in U.S. policy toward Cuba are greater today than ever before along the conflict between the two countries. The process that led to the presidential sanction of the Helms-Burton Law has once again shown that the ultra-right political sectors control U.S. anti-Cuban policy.

While since his participation in the 1992 electoral campaign, William Clinton gave signs his Administration was not prone to follow the same trend the preceding ones had followed toward Cuba, it is not less true that the high anti-Cuban consensus in U.S. society, the strength of conservative attitudes among the factors influencing U.S. policy toward Cuba, and the inconsistencies he has shown along his presidential term have turned him into a prisoner of a policy that has doubtlessly demonstrated its ineffectiveness to reach the strategic objectives of U.S. policy to "solve" the Cuban case for the last thirty nine years.

Under such circumstances, the Clinton administration policy toward Cuba instead of favoring the "pacific transition" in the Island—President Clinton's stated goal since the time he was a presidential candidate and adopted the postulates of the Law for Democracy in Cuba (the Torricelli Law)—has been forced to political actions that are contrary to the purpose in mind.

Since the Cold War ended, the main stated element of the policy the United States has been designing for the Island is the domestic Cuban reality—according to the U.S. point of view, once the Cold War finished, Cuba is no longer an antagonism-generating problem within the system of international relations that is fighting to establish itself.

Since the 1988 elections, it could be appreciated that the conditionings for a tactical change in U.S. policy toward Cuba were related to its politico-economic system. This argument has been reinforced.

Despite the prediction that Cuba would also be affected by the "domino theory"—and so it would collapse together with the socialist camp—failed noisily, the idea that it is necessary to revitalize the hostility policy as the only way to return the Island to the condition of a dependent territory, has been consolidating in the U.S. policy—such a return is a U.S. strategic goal, and it is considered the time is ripe to achieve it.

Precisely, that approach has been the basis for the anti-Cuban policy since 1988. Contrary to what might be expected from the considerations that the Cuban Revolution was the extension of the Soviet influence in America,

1. The Cuban revolutionary process survives—regardless the huge difficulties it is going through;

2. The economy has started a recovery process since 1995;

3. The openness to foreign capital is beginning to show its economy-spurring effects;

4. Actions to establish the articulation with the international economy have been initiated through bilateral agreements, and there are possibilities for multilateral economic agreements as well;

5. Cuban foreign policy results valid as a guarantor for its security before the United States in the international forums;

6. The internal political consensus maintains its capacity to make the political system feasible.

While from 1988 to 1992 the studies on Cuba were centered on predicting the time for—and the characteristics of—the collapse of the revolutionary project, since 1992 a significant turn started. Studies on Cuban reality commenced to point out the possibility of a pacific change in the Island even under Fidel Castro's leadership, and the need for the United States to adopt a respectful attitude before a significant set of transformations the Revolution has effected on Cuban society.

The increased number of political organizations in the ideologically moderate Cuban-American community which calls for national reconciliation is doubtlessly related to this phenomenon.

On its part, the so-called great U.S. press began to involve itself as never before in the Cuban debate from positions defending the replacement of aggressiveness as a basic component of the policy toward Cuba—especially the economic blockade.

The answer from the conservative political forces, instead of favoring the development of a policy toward Cuba based on the proposals to replace the aggressiveness, has only confirmed how slowly U.S. anti-Cuban policy is adjusted to realities.

The aggressive option to deal with Cuba is so deep-rooted in U.S. policy that it may even contradict the purpose of avoiding a "violent change" in the Island. But that is not alien to the course of the political thought in the United States

The Republican triumph in the 1994 mid-term congressional elections was the fanfare that announced the advance and enthronement of the most conservative positions of the traditional U.S. politico-ideological spectrum in the society.

It is evident that there is no room for nonconservative goals and participation in the process of shaping the post-Cold War world order, and in the disputes on how to solve U.S. economic, political, and social problems. The uncertainty feeling due to ignoring the role and place of the United States in the international arena in the future world order seems to lie in the substratum of that renovation of conservative positions.

Such a politico-ideological context is the ambit for the U.S. political forces in favor of the maximum hostility as the only political option toward Cuba, and it has forced a president—a little consistent one at that—to follow suit.

As it happened during the Carter administration —with due respect for the known differences—, President Clinton's interest in reelection forced him to join the run from conservative positions, and was trapped by the ultra-right factions in the policy towards Cuba.

The strength of the anti-Cuban right faction has been demonstrated whenever it has realized Cuba is able to impact U.S. policy—as to provoke at least a relaxation between the two countries—from the consolidation of its internal and international positions. Such a faction has capitalized on both artificially created crisis and real incidents.

In a national context marked by the triumph of political conservatism, a set of circumstances seem to be demanding the exercise of the leadership of the ultra-right anti-Cuban faction in the shaping process of the policy toward the Island to revert whatever actions that might modify the approach to the Cuban issue. In this sense, the following facts may be taken into account:

1. The signature of a Migration Accord between Cuba and the United States in September 1994—modified in May 1995—which solved the so-called crisis of the raftsmen—created by uncontrolled emigration of Cubans to the United States—and the establishment of serious mechanisms to its fulfillment are relevant because they grant legitimacy to the Cuban authorities, despite the reiterated statement that the Cuban regime is at the brink of collapsing.

2. The visits to Cuba of U.S. personalities in the last months of 1995 and the beginning of 1996—although those were private visits and nobody may categorically affirm or deny their purpose was to initiate an approach process between the two countries—would have seemed highly unlikely to occur years ago.[121]

3. The reiterated participation of the most influencing press on U.S. political circles and public opinion regarding the debate on the policy to follow toward Cuba. The fact the press questioned the economic blockade is a phenomenon without precedent in the history of Cuba-U.S. conflict for the last thirty-nine years.

4. Despite the issue of the Cuban compensations to U.S. companies nationalized in 1960 has maintained its presence in the U.S. agenda on its conflictive relations with Cuba, the position of the U.S. business

121. Among them, congressmen like Bill Richardson (New Mexico), deputy congressmen, and people very close to the high echelon of the Administration.

community is showing—as never before—a growing interest in participating in the opening of Cuban economy to foreign capital. Although the business community is still far from forming a political pressure group in favor of partially or totally lifting the blockade, it is no less true that it is making its interest in doing business with Cuba be felt. This community is questioning both the blockade policy and its tightening, and the notion is gaining room in public opinion.[122]

5. World resistance to follow the United States in its policy of subordinating Cuba via the economic blockade—especially the European Community, Latin America, Mexico, and Canada—cannot be compared to what happened when it was set up three decades ago. Not in vain, back in September 1992, an editorial in the *New York Times* qualified the approval by the General Assembly of the United Nations of the resolution condemning the U.S. blockade against Cuba as a humiliation to U.S. diplomacy.[123]

As a result of the above considerations, U.S. perception of the state of Cuba-U.S. relations has a two-direction effect. Among the conservatives, the sum and substance of the bilateral relations—what is going on in Cuba plus the Cuban debate within the United States—reinforces their will to leave no opportunity for Cuba to eventually come out of the crisis, hosting the independence banner, and even less to allow the conflict between the two countries to follow a course differing from the one they have set. On the other hand, those who favor the "pacific subversion" of the Island consider its resistance capacity

122. Refer to Carlos Batista, "Relaciones económicas entre Cuba y Estados Unidos a partir de 1959. Bloqueo y compensaciones." Typescript.
123. This resolution has been approved in successive periods of the General Assembly of the United Nations with an increasing number of votes in favor.

the confirmation that the feasible policy is the "political intervention." However, the latter keep on being too feeble to impact the course of the policy.

The most irrefutable example that the right continues to enjoy the leadership of the policy toward Cuba is expressed through the very process of approval of the Helms-Burton Law. As the right stamped the conservative mark on the candidates running for president in 1996, and taking into account the relevance of the Republican affiliation of the Congress, President Clinton had no alternative but signing the law. The incident concerning the planes shot down by the Cuban Air Force[124] was a fortuitous event that impacted the approval process of the law by the President. But it must not be considered as the ultimate cause for the decision. Had it not been the detonator, those interested in the law being passed would have found another incident of similar effects.

The approval process of the Helms-Burton Law also shows that on suspecting a potential approach between Cuba and the United States, the right leading the policy toward Cuba is able to erect obstacles—unsurmountable at least in the medium term—which can paralyze sectors promoting a different way to practice such a policy. On this occasion, a void on the governmental levels that conduct the policy toward Latin America also helped the triumph of the aggressiveness-prone positions.[125]

124. On February 24, 1996, the Cuban Air Force shot down two planes belonging to the counterrevolutionary group "Brothers at Rescue," which had penetrated the air space of the Island. This kind of provocations had been frequently happening during the previous months.
125. The signature of the Helms-Burton Law coincided with the departure from the Administration of a group of personalities that had occupied key positions in the policy toward Latin America—among them, Alexander Watson, deputy secretary of state for Latin America, and Richard Feinberg, counselor for Latin America in the National Security Council.

The outcome of the circumstances so far analyzed, consolidates regular trends in the U.S. policy toward Cuba :

1. The leadership belongs to the ultra-right.
2. Cuba-U.S. common interests—like the emigration issue—stress their capacity to find mutually adequate solutions through dialogue and negotiation.

But, on the other hand, new trends seem to be settling: The return to the essence of the Cuba-U.S. conflict—sovereignty versus hegemony—since 1990 has determined that the policy toward Cuba is not ruled by a set of regulations from diverse governmental levels but by laws—Torricelli Law in 1992, and Helms-Burton Law in 1996— which, like the latter, make the president play the role of an officer forced to account for his performance on a policy he has not promoted. This is a brand-new experience in the last half century. During the post-World War II period and as an imperative derived from the condition of being the leader of an strategic-military, politico-ideological, and economic bloc, the U.S. executive power enjoyed maximum prerogatives in the field of foreign policy. In that context, the prerogatives were gladly handed over by the Congress, but on the disappearance of the Communist enemy, it seems to be considering their recovery—as shown by the debate on the subject and the approval of the Helms-Burton Law.

The international context has evolved from being a preeminent factor in conditioning the Cuba-U.S. conflict until the Cold War ended, to playing a secondary role in the set of factors intervening in the referred conflict.

As it may be noticed since the late 1980s, the conflictive Cuba-U.S. relation has been limited to the conception that emerged in the last years of the 18th century, i.e., the exercise of U.S. hegemony over the Island against Cubans' will to make its condition of independent nation-state prevail.

Nowadays Cuba is disconnected from the main objective of U.S. foreign policy, which is focused on the course the North-North relations will take. These are predictably contradictory, and markedly detrimental to North-South links. Without having put into force the Helms-Burton Law, the United States is having difficulties with the rest of the countries in the world—including its big trade partners—due to its extraterritorial aspect. The rebuke wave the Law has set off, is based on the violation of the free-trade principle recognized as ineludible requirement of the future system of international economic relations.

Cuba has not been, is not, and will not be a priority for U.S. foreign policy. But for the last two centuries it has played a symbolic and/or functional role in the achievement of the strategic interests of the United States. From the proposals which are being promoted, it is indeed unquestionable that the treatment to the Cuban case would be trapped in considerations that would maintain the hostility pattern in all fronts. And that would become an obstacle to activate a reevaluation of the tools to apply to Cuba.

Within an internal context in which the most conservative politico-ideological positions are gaining ground, the chances for the rest of the factors involved in shaping the policy toward Cuba in the United States to make an impact on it in a different direction to the present one, are almost nonexistent.

The "silent majority" of the Cuban community settled in the United States—a majority fragmented and lacking the means to insert itself in the complex and costly U.S. political machinery— will continue to be a potential factor to influence a change. The cohesive element—the interest in normal relations between the two countries which allow such a majority to have stable links with its native country—will be disregarded by the current policy—a policy that will reinforce the role of the ultra-conservative wing of that community: the Cuban-American National Foundation.

The evidences of the close relation between the growing interest of U.S. businessmen and the active participation of the most important U.S. press—*New York Times, Wall Street Journal, Washington Post, Los Angeles Times*—in the debate on the course to be taken by the policy toward Cuba force a careful consideration on why those businessmen are interested in a relation with Cuba, and what is the scope of this business interest. Only when they realize they are losing real business opportunities—not potential opportunities as it used to be[126]—, will they form a political pressure group to foster a policy change—mainly regarding the economic blockade—from government levels.

On their part, the solidarity groups formed around the demand of lifting the blockade to Cuba will be able to make an impact on the U.S. policy toward the Island in the same measure they are favored by the internal context. Lacking autonomy as a policy factor, their actions are restricted to very precise limits.

In summary, the modifications of Cuba-U.S. relations in the context of the globalizing trends will be strengthened—at least in the medium and short terms—by the contradiction emerging from the North-South conflict. This conflict is aggravated by persisting patterns inherited from the Cold War era.

With the promulgation of the Helms-Burton Law, the U.S. policy toward Cuba has gained a new quality. From

126. Interview by Dr. Chailloux to executives of the División de Negocios con Estados Unidos of the Ministerio para la Inversión Extranjera y la Cooperación, August, 1995.

a presidential matter it has become a congressional pre-
rogative. Before a Congress dominated by the Republican right, the president must account for the application
of the postulates imposed upon him by that very same
organ. Consequently, the modification of the policy would
have to overcome the resistance of an organ whose
complexity not only derives from the number of people
and interests it consists of, but also from the anti-Cuban
consensus it is dominated by.

But not only the president is tied up as far as relaxing
the policy toward Cuba is concerned, so are those who
participate in the debate on the attitude to follow regarding Cuba from positions that disregard obstinate
hostility. The scope of the debate and the actions related
to the policy toward Cuba have been set within the most
rigid limits one might ever imagine. Thus, U.S. policy increases one of its more vulnerable sides: the incapacity
to timely adjust itself to the changes in the conflict dynamic.

A particular aspect of the future development of the
Cuba-U.S. conflict might be related to the potential advance of the new world institutionalization proposed by
the "center" countries. Likewise Cuba has traditionally
counted on an active participation in international forums to face U.S. hostility, U.S. demands for the Cuban
revolutionary project to surrender, if the United States is
defeated by the new conceptions in progress, might be
masked by the set of world trends presented as an international community consensus.

North countries' conditionings to grant aid and/or cooperation to South nations is a phenomenon dating
back to the last decade. A set of conceptions directed to
be implemented as to attain a harmonious exercise of
economic and political hegemony is in progress in international forums and institutions. Concepts like "good
governance," "limited sovereignty," "democracy," "hu-

man rights," "collective security," "humanitarian intervention," "peace maintenance" not only are gaining universal identity but also manifest themselves through the actions undertaken by diverse international forums on the assumption that they serve the interests of all nations alike, i.e., whether they belong to the North or to the South. The U.S. anti-Cuban policy might capitalize on these advances and consequently a new challenge for the Cuban national project of independence and sovereignty would be born.

Therefore, taking into account the characteristic complexity the Cuba-U.S. conflict is going through, it is necessary to estimate the influence the United States might be exercising over the Cuba-European Union relations. The contacts between U.S. political personalities and the European Union seem to indicate the former want to take advantage of one of the novel and distinctive trends of the globalization process.

Should the globalization political trends promoting the universalization of the western model progress, we will once again face the debasing of the true character of the hegemony vs sovereignty conflict. The situation then would resemble the existing one during the East-West confrontation, when the bilateral essence of the Cuba-U.S. conflict was obscured by the multilateral dimension.

The future development of the study that partially finishes here must continue by considering the influence of the globalization process in the Cuba-U.S. conflict. It will have to not only pay special attention to the centers' pretension to set up a worldwide cultural project but also to the internal realities of Cuba and the United States, for they are factors involved in the policy of one country relative to the other. In such a future study, the political and institutional practice will receive special notice due to their potential repercussion on Cuban reality.

Until then let us keep on closely watching the development of the new world trends to correct the course of our understanding of the reality, and to aid the construction of a Cuban society project in which the autochthonous and the universal angles help consolidate our condition of being a factor that contributes to the enrichment of human society—a one and diverse human society. To attain such a goal it would be a good idea to turn a José Martí's postulate into a law: "Salvation lies in creating. Creating is the password for this generation"[127] because "serious issues are not solved by preconceived theories."[128]

127. José Martí, "Nuestra América," in *Obras completas*, vol. 6 (La Habana: Editorial Nacional de Cuba, 1963-1965), 18.
128. Martí, "El proletariado de Castillo Velasco," ibid., 345.

Bibliography

Agresiones de Estados Unidos a Cuba. 1787-1976. La Habana: Editorial de Ciencias Sociales, 1979.

Albert, Michel. *Capitalismo contra capitalismo.* Buenos Aires: Paidós, 1992.

Amin, Samir. "El futuro de la polarización global." *Realidad Económica,* no. 130 (1995).

Arroyo, G. "La globalización como caos." *Capítulos,* no. 36 (July-Sept. 1993).

Art, Robert J. "A Defensible Defense: America's Grand Strategy After the Cold War." *International Security* 15 (4) (Spring 1991).

Asamblea Nacional del Poder Popular. *Proyecto de modificaciones a la Constitución de la República,* La Habana.

Asmus, Ronald D., Richard L. Kluger, and F. Stephen Larrabe. "Building a New NATO." *Foreign Affairs* 72 (4) (Sept.-Oct. 1993).

Asmus, Ronald D. *The New U.S. Strategic Debate. Prepared for the United States Army.* Santa Monica: Rand, 1993.

Banco Mundial. "Informe sobre el desarrollo humano 1994." *The World Bank* (1994).

_____. "Informe sobre el desarrollo mundial, 1989. Los sistemas financieros y el desarrollo." *The World Bank* (1989).

Baró Herrera, Silvio. "La cláusula social." *Trabajadores* (May 1994).

_____. "Derechos humanos, desarrollo y Nuevo Orden Mundial." *Informes Especiales-Centro de Estudios Europeos* (December 1994).

_____. "El desarrollo sostenible: desafío para la humanidad" (1995). Typescript.

_____. "Globalización y exclusión: dos tendencias en la economía mundial" (May 1992). Typescript.

_____. *El nuevo orden económico internacional: antecedentes, problemas actuales y perspectivas.* La Habana: Editorial de Ciencias Sociales, 1980.

_____. "Las relaciones Norte-Sur a cincuenta años de la Conferencia de Bretton Woods." *Revista de Estudios Europeos,* no. 31, 1994.

Batista, Carlos. "Relaciones económicas de Cuba y Estados Unidos a partir de 1959. Bloqueo y compensaciones." Typescript.

Bendesky, L. "La dimensión del proceso entre globalización económica." *Problemas del Desarrollo* 24 (95) (Oct.-Dec. 1993).

Berger, Thomas U. "From Sword to Chrysantemum: Japan's Culture of Anti-Militarism." *International Security* 15 (4) (Spring 1991).

Bhagwati, Jagdish. *Regionalization and Multilateralism: An Overview*. World Bank and CEPR Conference on New Dimension in Regional Integration, Session I, Paper no. 1, Washington, D.C.

Bitar, Sergio, and Colin I. Bradford, Jr. *Strategic Options for Latin America in the 1990s*. Paris: Centro de Desarrollo de la OCDE and Banco Interamericano de Desarrollo, 1992.

Bloomfield, Richard J., and Gregory Treverton, eds. *Alternatives to Intervention: A New U.S. Latin-American Security Relationship*. Boulder, Colo.: Lynne Rienner Publishers, Inc., 1990.

Bondarerski, B., and V. Sofinski. *La no alineación: sus amigos y adversarios en la política mundial*. Moscú: Ciencias Sociales Contemporáneas, 1979.

Boutros-Ghali, Boutros. "A New Departure on Development." *Foreign Policy*, no. 98 (Spring 1995).

_____. *Un programa para paz*. Nueva York: Naciones Unidas, 1992.

Bradford, Colin I., Jr. "Tendencias y problemas de la regionalización y nuevo orden internacional." *Capítulos*, no. 36 (July-Sept. 1993).

Brawley, Mark A. *Liberal Leadership: Great Powers and Their Challengers in Peace and War*. Nueva York: Cornell University Press, 1993.

Buchman, Harry M. *U.S. Security in the Twenty-First Century*. Boulder, Colo.: Westview Press, Inc. 1987.

Butter, Shawn. "Regional Security after the Cold War. Conference Report." *Working Paper - Center for Iberian and Latin American Studies (CILAS)*, no. 4 (November 1993).

Brzezinski, Zbigniew. *Out of Control: Global Turmoil on the Eve of the 21st Century*. New York: Charles Scribner's Son, 1993.

_____. "The Premature Partnership." *Foreign Affairs* 73 (1) (Jan.-Feb. 1994).

Castro, Fidel. *La crisis económica y social del mundo. Informe a la VII Cumbre de los Países No Alineados*. La Habana: Oficina de Publicaciones del Consejo de Estado, 1983.

Castro Mariño, Soraya et al. "La política norteamericana hacia Cuba en 1995." CESEU-UH, La Habana, November 1995. Typescript.

Ceceña, Ana Esther. "Sobre las diferentes modalidades de internacionalización del capital." *Problemas del Desarrollo* 21 (81) (April-June 1990).

CEPAL. *Balance preliminar de la economía de América Latina y el Caribe* (1993).

Bibliography

Chailloux Laffita, Graciela. "La fuerza de los intereses comunes en las relaciones cubano-norteamericanas." *Cuban Review*, no. 1 (November 1994).

Christopher, Warren. "America's Leadership, America's Opportunity." *Foreign Policy*, no. 98 (Spring 1995).

Collingsworld, F., William Goald, and Pharis F. Harvey. "Time for a Global New Deal." *Foreign Affairs* 73 (1) (Jan.-Feb. 1994).

Comisión del Sur. *Desafío para el Sur*, México: Fondo de Cultura Económica, 1991.

Commission on Global Governance. *Our Global Neigbourhood*. Geneva, 1993.

Congressional Research Service. *U.S. Power in a Changing World. A Report Prepared for the Subcommittee on International Economic Policy and Trade of the Committee on Foreign Affairs, U.S. House of Representatives*. Washington, D.C.: U. S. Government Printing Office, 1990.

Cowhey, Peter, and Jonathan D. Aronson. "A New Trade Order." *Foreign Affairs* (America and the World, 1992/1993).

Dainsai, C., ed. *La tercera revolución industrial*. Buenos Aires: Grupo Editorial Latinoamericano, 1988.

David, Steven R. "Why the Third World Still Matters." *International Security* 17 (3) (Winter 1992/1993).

Deibel, Terry L. "Strategies before Containment: Patterns for the Future." *International Security* 18 (3) (Spring 1992).

De Melo, Jaime, and Arvind Panagariya. "The New Regionalism in Trade Policy." *The World Bank* (September 21, 1992).

De Melo, Jaime, and Sumanna Dhor. "Lessons in Trade Liberalization in Latin America for Economies in Transition." *The World Bank*, Working Paper no. WPS 1040 (November, 1992).

De Melo, Jaime and Arvind Panagariya, and Dani Rodrick. "The New Regionalism: A Country Perspective." *The World Bank*, Working Paper no. WPS 1094 (February 1993).

Department of Defense. *Defense Strategy for the 1990s: The Regional Defense Strategy*. Washington, D.C., 1993.

Dole, Robert. "Shaping America's Global Future." *Foreign Policy*, no. 98 (Spring 1995).

Dunning, John H. *Globalization, Economic Restructuring and Development*. Geneva: UNCTAD, 1994.

Eden, Lynn. "The End of the Cold War History?" *International Security* 18 (1) (Summer 1993).

Fernández Tabío, Luis René. "La cumbre de las Américas: ¿una nueva política económica para América Latina?" Typescript.

Fieleke, Norman. "One Trading World or Many: The Issue of Regional Trading Blocs." *New England Economic Review* (May-June 1992).

FMI. *Ventajas de la liberación de los controles de capital,* Washington, D.C. (April 12, 1993).

Fontela, Emilio. "European Economic Integration in a Long-Term Perspective." In *Long-Term Prospect for the World Economy.* Paris: OCDE, 1992.

Friedberg, Aaronl. "Why Didn't the United States Become a Garrison State?" *International Security* 16 (4) (Spring 1992).

Funabashi, Y., Michel Oksenberg, and Heinrich Weiss. *An Emerging China in a World of Interdependence: A Report to the Trilateral Commission.* New York: The Trilateral Commission, 1994.

Furtado, Celso. *Economía mundial. Transformación y crisis.* Colombia: Tercer Mundo Editores, 1990.

Gaddis, John L. "International Relations Theory and the End of the Cold War" *International Security* 17 (3) (Winter 1992-1993).
_____. "The Tragedy of Cold War History." *Foreingn Affairs* 73 (1) (Jan.-Feb. 1994*).*

Garza, A. de la. "Globalización de la política." *Relaciones Internacionales,* no. 52 (1991).

Gause, F. Gregory, III. "The Illogic of Dual Containment." *Foreign Affairs* 73 (2) (March-April 1994).

Glaser, Charles L. "Why NATO is Still Best: Future Security Arrangements for Europe." *International Security* 18 (1) (Summer 1993).

González, G. "Notas sobre la geopolítica y el nacionalismo." *Relaciones Internacionales,* no. 52 (1991).

González Sousa, Roberto, and Pablo E. Chaviano Núñez. "Economía y medio ambiente, algunas consideraciones metodológicas." *Investigaciones sobre medio ambiente.* FLACSO-Cuba/SODEPAZ, 1993.

Gorostiaga, Xabier. "América Latina frente a los desafíos globales." In *Estado, Nuevo Orden Económico y Democracia en América Latina.* Caracas: Editorial Nueva Sociedad, 1992.

Guerra-Borges, Alfredo. "Repercusiones previsibles del mercado único europeo en América Latina y el Caribe." *Comercio Exterior* 42 (8) (August 1992).

Gunder Frank, André. "El desarrollo del subdesarrollo," *Cuadernos Anagrama,* (1971).

Guillén, Arturo R. "Bloques regionales y globalización de la economía." *Comercio Exterior* 44 (5) (May 1994).

Hamilton, Lee H. "A Democrat Looks at Foreign Policy." *Foreign Policy* (Summer 1992).

Harris, Owen. "The Collapse of 'The West'." *Foreign Affairs* 72 (4) (Sept.-Oct. 1993).

Hendrickson, David C. "The Recovery of Internationalism." *Foreign Affairs* 73 (5) (Sept.-Oct. 1994).

Holmes, Kim R. "Bush's New World Order: What's Wrong with This Picture?" *The Heritage Lectures*, no. 333 (1991).

Homer-Dixon, Thomas F. "On the Threshold: Environmental Changes as Causes of Acute Conflict." *International Security* 16 (2) (Fall 1991).

Horowitz, Evely. "Los retos del sistems de comercio mundial." Capítulos , no. 36 (July-Sept. 1993).

House of Representatives. *The Future of U.S. Foreign Policy in the Post Cold War Era. Hearings before the Committee on Foreign Affairs.* 102nd Cong., 2nd sess. February 6, 19, 20; March 5, 24; and April 30, 1992. Washington, D.C.: U.S. Government Printing Office, 1992.

Hufbaner, Gary C. "Las perspectivas del comercio mundial en los noventa y sus implicaciones para los países en desarrollo." *Pensamiento Iberoamericano* (July-Dec. 1991).

Huntington, Samuel P. "The Clash of Civilizations?" *Foreign Affairs* 72 (3) (Summer 1993).

_____. *La tercera ola. La democratización a finales del siglo XX.* Buenos Aires: Paidós 1994.

_____. "Why International Primacy Matters." *International Security* 17 (4) (Spring 1993).

Icaza, Carlos A. de, and José Rivera Banuel. *El orden mundial emergente: México en el siglo XXI.* México: Consejo Nacional para la Cultura y las Artes, 1994.

Iglesias, Enrique V. *Reflections on Economic Development: Toward a New Latin American Consciouness.* Washington: Inter-American Development Bank, 1992.

Institute for Defense *Analysis. American Security in an Interdependent World. A Collection of Papers to the Atlantic Council's 1987 Annual Conference.* Laham: University Press of America, 1988.

Institute of International Politics and Economics. *Non-Alignment in the Eighties.* Belgrade, 1982.

IRELA. *Cuba en crisis: Procesos y perspectivas.* Madrid, 1994.

Jackson, Robert H., and Alan James. *States in a Changing World: A Contemporary Analysis.* New York: Oxford University Press, Inc., 1993.

Jaguaribe, Helio. "La relación Norte-Sur." *Revista de Estudios Internacionales* (1990).

Jenks, Leland H. *Nuestra colonia de Cuba.* La Habana: Edición Revolucionaria, 1966.

Jervis, Robert. "International Primary: Is the Game Worth the Candle?" *International Security* 17 (4) (Spring 1993).

Katzenstein, Peter J., and Nobuo Okawara. "Japan's National Security." *International Security* 17 (4) (Spring 1993).

Kegley, Charles W., Jr., and Gregory A. Raymond. *A Multipolar Peace?: Great-Power Politics in the 21st Century*. New York: San Martin Press, 1994.

Kennedy, Paul. *Preparing for the Twenty First Century*. New York: Random House, 1993.

_____. *The Rise and Fall of the Great Powers*. New York: Random House, 1989.

Kliksberg, Bernardo, comp. *El rediseño del Estado: una perspectiva internacional*. México: Fondo de Cultura Económica, 1994.

Krugman, Paul. "Competitiveness: a Dangerous Obsession." *Foreign Affairs* 73 (2) (March-April 1994).

_____. *Geography and Trade*. Cambridge: MIT Press, 1991.

_____. "Towards a Counter-Counter-Revolution in Development Theory." In *World Bank Annual Conference on Development Economics*. Washington, D.C.: The World Bank, 1992.

Lake, Anthony. "Confronting Backlash States." *Foreign Affairs* 73 (2) (March-April 1994).

Laqueur, Walter. "Save Public Diplomacy." *Foreign Affairs* 73 (5) (Sept.-Oct. 1994).

Layne, Christopher. "The Unipolar Illusion: Why New Great Powers Will Rise." *International Security* 17 (4) (Spring 1993).

Le Riverend, Julio. *Historia económica de Cuba*. La Habana: Editorial de Ciencias Sociales, 1985.

Lenin, V. I. *El imperialismo, fase superior del capitalismo*. Moscú: Editorial Progreso, n.d.

López Civeira, Francisca, comp. *Historia de las relaciones de EE.UU. con Cuba*. La Habana, Ministerio de Educación Superior, 1985.

López Oceguera, Rosa. "Cuba en el debate político norteamericano: ¿hacia un nuevo consenso?" *Visión USA* (Jan. 1994).

_____ . "Estados Unidos en tres Cumbres." *Visión USA* (Dec. 1994).

_____. "La guerra fría: contexto general de la relación triangular Cuba/EE.UU./URSS." CESE-UUH, 1993. Typescript.

_____. "Implicaciones políticas del proyecto de Ley Helms-Burton." *Visión USA* (May 1995).

_____. "La relación Cuba-Estados Unidos en la problemática Norte/Sur." *Visión USA* (Jan. 1995).

Luttwak, Edward N. "From Geopolitics to Geoeconomics: Logic of Conflict, Grammar of Commerce." *The National Interest* (Summer 1990).

McGrew, A. G., and P.G. Lewis, eds. *Global Politics: Globalization and the Nation State*. Cambridge: The Polity Press, 1992.

Maira, Luis. "América Latina frente a los desafíos del nuevo sistema internacional." *Diálogo y Seguridad*, no. 1 (Dec. 1994).

Bibliography

Martí, José. "Nuestra América" In *Obras completas,* vol 6. La Habana: Editorial Nacional de Cuba, 1963-1965.

——————. "El proletariado de Castillo Velasco." In *Obras completas,* vol. 6. La Habana: Editorial Nacional de Cuba, 1963-1965.

Mastanduno, Michael. "Do Relative Gains Matter?: America´s Response to Japanese Industrial Policy." *International Security* 16 (1) (Summer 1991).

Meadows, Dorella et al. *Los límites del crecimiento. Informe al Club de Roma.* México: Fondo de Cultura Económica, 1981.

Mesarovic, Mihailo, and Eduard Pestel. *La humanidad en la encrucijada. Informe al Club de Roma.* México: Fondo de Cultura Económica, 1975.

Minsburg, Naúm, and H. V. Valle, eds. *El impacto de la globalización: la encrucijada económica del siglo XXI.* Buenos Aires: Ediciones Letra Buena, 1994.

Moneta, Carlos Juan. "Los probables escenarios de la globalización." *Capítulos,* no. 36 (Jul.-Sept. 1993).

Motta Velga, Pedro da. "Los nuevos condicionantes internacionales de la competitividad." *Capítulos,* no. 36 (Jul.-Sept. 1993).

Mullin, Keith. "Playing the Regional Card." In *IFR Inter-American Development Bank Report.* Washington, D.C., March 1993.

Ohmae, Kiniche. *Triad Power. The Coming Shape of Global Competition.* New York: Free Press, 1985.

Olave, Patricia. "América Latina frente al bloque comercial estadounidense." *Problemas del Desarrollo* 24 (95) (Oct.-Dec. 1993).

Oman, Charles. "Globalización: la nueva competencia." *Capítulos,* no. 36 (Jul.-Sept. 1993).

Ominami, C., ed. *Estudio económico y social del mundo 1994.* New York: United Nations, 1994.

——————. *Informe acerca de la situación social del mundo 1993.* New York: United Nations, 1993.

——————. *La tercera revolución industrial.* Buenos Aires: Grupo Editorial Latinoamericano, 1986.

——————. *World Investment Report 1992.* New York: United Nations, 1992.

ONU. *Informe de la Comisión Mundial sobre el Medio Ambiente y el Desarrollo (Nuestro futuro común).* Document A/42/427. Nueva York, 1987.

Ornelas Bernal, Raúl. *Inversión extranjera y reconvención industrial.* México: Instituto de Investigaciones Económicas, UNAM, 1991.

Partido Comunista de Cuba. "Resolución sobre política exterior." In *IV Congreso del PCC, discursos y documentos.* La Habana: Editora Política, 1992.

Pastor, Robert A. "Preempting Revolutions: The Boundaries of U.S. Influence." *International Security* 15 (4) (Spring 1991).

Picco, Giandomenico. "The U.N. and the Use of Force." *Foreign Affairs* 73 (2) (March-April 1994).

PNUD. *Algunas preguntas y respuestas sobre el desarrollo humano sostenible.* S. L., 1994.

—————. *Informe de desarrollo humano, 1990.* Bogotá: Tercer Mundo Editores, 1990.

—————. *Informe de desarrollo humano, 1992.* Bogotá: Tercer Mundo Editores, 1992.

—————. *Informe de desarrollo humano, 1994.* México: Fondo de Cultura Económica, 1994.

Pronk, Jan, and Mabub ul Haq. *The Hague Report: Sustainable Development from Concept to Actions.* S. L., 1992.

Ramamurthy, K., and Govind Narain Srivastava. *NAM Today.* Institute for Non-Aligned Studies, 1985.

Ramírez López, Berenice P. "América Latina frente al proceso de globalización: retos y potencialidades." *Problemas del Desarrollo* 24 (95) (Oct.-Dec. 1993).

Rangel, J. "Estados Unidos: hegemonía versus globalización." *Capítulos,* no. 36 (Jul.-Sept. 1993).

Raymond, S. "La desaparición del Tercer Mundo." *Reforma Económica Hoy,* no. 4 (1994).

Reich, Robert. *The World of Nations: Preparing Ourselves for 21st Century Capitalism.* New York: Alfred A. Knopf, n.d.

Risse-Kappen, Thomas. "Did ´Peace Though´ End the Cold War?: Lessons from INF." *International Security* 16 (1) (Summer 1991).

Rodríguez, Carlos Rafael. "Fundamentos estratégicos de la Revolución Cubana." In *Letra con Filo,* vol 1. La Habana: Editorial de Ciencias Sociales, 1983.

Rojas, Francisco. "From War to Integration: Democratic Transition and Security Issues." In *Redefining National Security in Latin America. Workshop Report,* Woodrow Wilson Center, November 16-17, 1992. The Latin American Program no. 204.

Rosecrance, Richard, and Arthur A. Stein, eds. *The Domestic Bases of Grand Strategy.* New York: Cornell University Press, 1993.

Roseman, James. *Turbulence and World Politics. A Theory of Change and Continuity.* Princeton University Press, 1990.

Rostow, Walt Whitman. *Política y etapas de crecimiento.* Barcelona: Dopesa, 1972.

—————. *The Stages of Economic Growth. A Non-Communist Manifesto.* Cambridge Univesity Press, 1962.

Sach, Jeffrey D. "Consolidating Capitalism." *Foreign Policy,* no. 98 (Spring 1995).

Bibliography

Sauvant, Karl P. *El Grupo de los 77: evolución, estructura, organización.* La Habana: Ministerio de Comercio Exterior, n.d.

Shoultz, Lars. "Inter-American Security: The Changing Perceptions of U.S. Policy Makers." (April 26-28, 1990). Mimeo.

Sebenius, James K. "Designing Negotiations toward a New Regime: The Case of Global Warning." *International Security* 15 (4) (Spring 1991).

SELA. "El Acuerdo General sobre Comercio de Servicios (GATS): importancia y oportunidades para la región latinoamericana." SELA, Caracas, SP/CL/XIX.O/Di, no. 3 (1994).

————. "Resultados de las negociaciones comerciales multilaterales de la Ronda Uruguay, SELA." Caracas, SP/CL/XX.O/Di, no. 2 (1994).

SELA/UNCTAD. *Comercio y medio ambiente: el debate internacional.* Caracas: Editorial Nueva Sociedad, 1995.

Serafino, Nina. "U.S. Security Policy for Latin America and the Caribbean: Current Situation and Prospects." In *Redefining National Security in Latin America: Workshop Report,* Woodrow Wilson Center, November 16-17, 1992, The Latin American Program no. 204.

Sivard, Ruth Leger. *World Military Expenditures 1993.* Washington, D.C., 1993.

Stanic, Slavko. *La no alineación y el nuevo orden económico internacional.* Belgrado: Cuestiones Actuales del Socialismo, 1979.

Steil, Beun. "Social Correctness is the New Protectionism." *Foreign Affairs* 73 (1) (Jan.-Feb. 1994).

Thurow, Lester. *Head to Head: The Coming Economic Battle among Japan, Europe and America.* New York: William Morrow and Co., 1992.

Tinbergen, Jan, and others. *Reshaping the International Order. A Report to the Club of Rome.* New York: Dutton, 1976.

Toro Hardy, Alfredo. "Globalización y caos." *Capítulos,* no. 36 (Jul.-Sept. 1993).

Torre, Augusto de la, and Margaret R. Kelly. "Regional Trade Arrangement." In *International Monetary Fund Occasional,* Paper no. 93 (March 1992). Washington D.C.: International Monetary Fund.

Vargas, Augusto. "Workshop Introduction." In *Redefining National Security in Latin America. Workshop. Report.* Woodrow Wilson Center, November 16-17, 1992. The Latin American Program no. 204.

Vidal Villa, J. M. "Diez tesis sobre la mundialización." *Memoria* (México) (Jan.-Feb. 1995).

Wayman, Frank W., and Paul F. Diehl. *Reconstructing Realpolitik.* The University of Michigan Press, 1994.

Weiner, Myron. "Security, Stability and Intertional Migration." *International Security* 17 (3) (Winter 1992-1993).

World Bank. *World Debt Tables 1992-1993*. Washington, D.C.: The World Bank, 1993.

——————. *World Development Report*. Oxford: University Press, 1993.

Yilmaz, Akyuz. "On Financial Openness in Delevopment Countries." *In International Monetary and Financial Issues for the 1990s*, vol. 2. UNCTAD, Research Papers for the G-24, New York, 1993.

Zakaria, Farceed. "Realism and Domestic Politics." *International Security* 17 (1) (Summer 1992).

Zakheim, Dov S., and Jeffrey M. Ranney. "Matching Defense Strategies to Resources: Challenges for the Clinton Administration." *International Security* 18 (1) (Summer 1993).

Zamerman, H. "Sobre bloqueo histórico y utopía en América Latina." *Problemas del Desarrollo* 24 (95) (Oct.-Dec. 1993).

Zaragoza, José. "La desmaterialización del trabajo y la reestructuración productiva capitalista." *Momento Económico*, no. 54 (1991).

——————. "El papel de los servicios en la reestructuración industrial" *Problemas del Desarrollo* 24 (95) (Oct.-Dec. 1993).